BUFFALO NATION

History and Legend of the North American Bison

Good things I am bringing, something holy to your nation.
A message I carry for your people from the Buffalo Nation.
—Greeting of the White Buffalo Woman, *Ptesan-Wi*,
upon her appearance to the Lakota Sioux

Valerius Geist

With Native North American legends and pictographs as well as writing and art from George Catlin, Crazy Horse, Sitting Bull, Mari Sandoz, Charles M. Russell, Albert Bierstadt, "Buffalo Bill" Cody, Gen. George Armstrong Custer, and many others.

Voyageur Press

Edited by Jane McHughen Publishing Services and Michael Dregni
Photograph and illustration research by Todd R. Berger and Michael Dregni
Designed by Andrea Rud
Printed in Hong Kong

First hardcover edition
96 97 98 99 00 5 4 3 2 1
First softcover edition
02 03 04 05 06 6 5 4 3 2

Library of Congress Cataloging-in-Publication Data
Geist, Valerius.
Buffalo nation : history and legend of the North American bison / by Valerius Geist.
p. cm.
Includes bibliographical references (p. 137) and index.
ISBN 0-89658-313-9
ISBN 0-89658-390-2 (pbk.)
1. American bison. 2. American bison hunting—History. 3. American bison—Folklore. 4. Indians of North America—Folklore. I. Title.
QL737.U53G435 1996
599.73'58—dc20 96-218
CIP

Published by Voyageur Press, Inc.
123 North Second Street, P.O. Box 338, Stillwater, MN 55082 U.S.A.
612-430-2210, fax 612-430-2211

Permissions

Page 1: *The snow-encrusted face of a North American bison. (Photo © Michael H. Francis)*

Pages 2–3: *A herd of buffalo graze the prairie grasses of Yellowstone National Park. (Photo © Tom Murphy)*

Page 3, inset: *Blackfoot Indian buffalo pictograph with heartline.*

Facing page: *Cowpoke Verne Elliott rides a bejewelled buffalo during a rodeo at Cheyenne, Wyoming's Frontier Days in 1910.*

Contents

Dedication

To Rosemarie, Karl, and Harold

Acknowledgments

I am grateful to the warden service and certain senior administrators of Canada's national parks for access to bison and to research material. I am grateful to my colleagues Dr. Ludwig Carbyn of the Canadian Wildlife Service; Dr. Mary Maegher, biologist and long-time student of bison, Yellowstone National Park; Peter Karsten, artist and retired director of the Calgary Zoo; Dr. Dale Lott, University of California at Davis; Joe Kimball, biologist, Wichita Mountain Wildlife Reserve; Professors John Foster and Ian S. MacLaren of the Department of English, University of Alberta; Karen M. McCullough, editor of *Arctic*, Calgary; Dr. Patricia A. McCormack of the Provincial Museum of Alberta, Edmonton; Bob Ruttan, old-time biologist; Dr. Guenther G. Sehm, Hamburg, and Wolfgang Frey, Gemering, Germany; Dr. Ian McTaggart-Cowan for review of earlier material; and my former student Bruce Greenfield for his generous assistance. I am deeply grateful for the patience, advice, and humor of my long-suffering wife, Renate Geist.

LONE BUFFALO
With its breath hanging in the winter air, a lone buffalo stands guard against a rock ledge at Yellowstone National Park. (Photo © Michael H. Francis)

Preface

THE BUFFALO: SYMBOL OF NORTH AMERICA

My first objective was to produce a coin which was truly American, and that could not be confused with the currency of any other country. I made sure, therefore, to use none of the attributes that other nations had used in the past. And, in my search for symbols, I found no motif within the boundaries of the United States so distinctive as the American buffalo.

—James Earle Fraser, designer of the U.S. buffalo nickel, 1913

BUFFALO NICKEL
Created by designer James Earle Fraser in the 1910s, the United States buffalo nickel featured an Indian's profile on the front side and this famous bison on the reverse. With the near-extermination of the bison by the U.S. government, "In God We Trust" took on new meaning. (Photo © Michael H. Francis)

The buffalo is a symbol of North America, but it is a symbol with many levels and hidden, deeper meanings.

Looking back some 300,000 years ago to the Ice Ages, the bison is one of several animal species that came to North America from Asia and survived to become part of the continent's "natural fauna."

But the "natural history" of the buffalo, like that of many animals from wolves to deer, is not truly *natural* in the strict sense of the word. The bison has been shaped by animal as well as human predators, from Paleo-Indians to Native North Americans to the arrival of the Europeans and their concept of "civilizing" the West.

In the mid-1800s, the fledgling United States waged war on the buffalo. The U.S. government and its army sought to exterminate the bison as part of an effort to push the Indians onto reservations and open the Wild West to settlers. With buffalo hunters as its right hand, the army aimed to destroy the buffalo as a source of food and spiritual power to the Native Americans. By 1883, the war was "won."

In Canada at the same time, the government aimed to assimilate Native People and settle them on reserves. Nonetheless, buffalo were extirpated on the Canadian plains just as effectively as in the United States. But the source of the bison's decimation in Canada was more economic than political: Buffalo were seen by the wealthy fur-trading companies as a commodity to be harvested.

By the dawn of the 1900s, movements to conserve wildlife from the onrush of civilization budded in the United States and Canada, and the plight of the bison was seen as a cause to rally behind. Over the last century, the bison was saved from the brink of extinction, and today it stands for a system of wildlife conservation that, although fraught with problems, is the most successful in the world.

But the future of the buffalo—as well as the future for us all—is far from secure.

BUFFALO AT SUNRISE
Silhouetted against the rising sun, a buffalo bull stands on a hill in Yellowstone National Park. (Photo © Alan and Sandy Carey)

Humans and bison still face the onrush of civilization, depletion of our natural resources, and a shrinking world.

The buffalo is a symbol of failures and successes. Its history provides lessons to be studied and hope that we can move forward to healing our planet.

Introduction

WILD THINGS IN WILD PLACES

O, give me a home where the buffalo roam,
Where the deer and the antelope play,
Where seldom is heard a discouraging word,
And the skies are not cloudy all day.
—Brewster Higley, *Home on the Range*, 1873

WHERE THE BUFFALO ROAM
A lone buffalo endures winter. (Photo © Michael H. Francis)

The bison appeared calm, even with two wolves following their every move. A few bison rested and chewed their cud, some fed, but most were just standing. A young bull stared at the two waiting wolves; six calves lay protected well within the herd. A gentle summer breeze ruffled the water of the shallow lake and rustled the leaves of the trees; peace and tranquillity appeared to reign over the twenty-seven bison, the two wolves, the green sedge meadow, the aspen bluffs, and the large, reedy lake. It was a mid-summer day, deep in Wood Buffalo National Park, Canada.

Dr. Ludwig Carbyn and I had watched the nursery herd the previous day. It was led by a dark-colored female with a crooked horn and a large beard. The bison had moved little during the night. Despite the peaceful scene, we kept our binoculars trained closely on the wolves and bison. We were hunched down about three hundred paces from them, screened by small aspens. The gray wolf got up, stretched and yawned, glanced at the bison and then, head held low and nose close to the ground, trotted off into the aspen forest. The large, light-colored wolf remained resting a little longer, but then also rose and walked slowly into the forest. The bison seemed to pay no attention.

The minutes ticked by. Suddenly the lead cow became alert. She glanced about nervously and tested the wind. The herd rose. For a brief moment the bison came together, heads elevated, fully alert, a compact mass. Then the lead cow was off at a quick walk. The others followed in single file. In a minute the herd was on the move. Only then did we notice, trailing at the rear, a limping cow and calf. The wolves must have attacked the herd since we saw them the preceding evening, and injured these two bison. As I swung my field glasses to where the bison herd had been seconds ago, I saw the light-colored wolf. It was crouched at the edge of the forest, its gaze fixed on the limping bison. And so it remained until the last bison disappeared into the forest. The wolf ran forward and sniffed the ground where the bison had rested. Then, glancing once over its shoulder after the bison, it trotted off in the opposite direction.

Dr. Carbyn and I walked back to the observation tower a couple of miles away

Buffalo cow and nursing calf
A young calf nurses while its mother stands guard against wolves at Wood Buffalo National Park in Alberta and the Northwest Territories of Canada. This Canadian national park contains the largest natural bison herd and, despite misadventures in management, has preserved the largest gene pool of the species Bison bison. *(Photo © L. N. Carbyn)*

in the middle of a large prairie. From here visibility was excellent for well over a mile in all directions and we could observe without intruding on the daily life of bison and wolves. We settled down and surveyed the scene. In a distant depression to the north, a wet sedge meadow, we saw well-dispersed dark dots. This was a group of feeding bison bulls. They were on a rich forage site, but the ground was soft and the bulls sank deep into the mud. Directly opposite to the south was another group of bulls, equally well spaced, also feeding in a wet sedge meadow. There were a few lone bulls scattered along the forested edge of the prairie, each in a wet pocket of lush sedges. No female bison were in sight.

Suddenly, a small herd of bison emerged in close single file from the forest and moved rapidly across the prairie. It was the herd we had observed earlier. The bison walked fast, visibly agitated. On the dry prairie their hooves raised clouds of dust that obscured the trailing members of the herd.

A black bear appeared out of a dip and ambled across the path of the bison. The lead cow stopped. She raised her head high, staring at the bear. The herd bunched behind her. Slowly, bison tails rose into the air. Time stopped. Then the bison charged. The bear lit out for the forest. The bison, densely packed, were gaining on the bear, which was running flat out in long bounds. It reached the forest ahead of the bison, paused, looked back at the approaching mass of dark bodies and dust, and dove for cover. The bison slowed down and stopped. They relaxed. The lead cow walked off in the direction she was following earlier. The herd fell into single file behind her.

On that afternoon in Wood Buffalo National Park, Dr. Carbyn and I witnessed bison security strategy, observed the different habitat choices of bulls and cows as the two sexes pursued different reproductive strategies, and saw bison charge a black bear—a sight few people have ever seen or will ever see.

What I had witnessed I owed to somebody, who, long before I was born, had labored to preserve buffalo for their children and their children's children. I was one of the unborn for whose sake members of the American Bison Society, and so many others, had worked hard and diligently to conserve the bison.

These conservationists acted as if the future was not a hypothesis, but a reality, and they believed that what they cared for should be available to people they would never meet. Without them, there would be no Wood Buffalo National Park, no Yellowstone National Park—no wilderness for bison, wolves, and bears. Without them, we would know as little of buffalo as we know of the dodo, great auk, or passenger pigeon. Much of the boreal forest and aspen bluffs through which these northern bison now roam would have been logged. Some of the land would have been converted to cattle pasture and fenced by barbed wire. There would be strip mines with heavy machinery noisily excavating gypsum, and perhaps a mining town or two.

Globally, wild lands under public stewardship and accessible to all are appreciating in value as wealth and employment are created by the demands of those who come to visit, explore, fish and, occasionally, hunt. A controversial new indus-

Wild things in wild places

A buffalo bull nonchalantly crosses a dirt road, paying no heed to traffic signs. Bison and roads may get along too well, as shown in Yellowstone National Park recently. Opening the park to snowmobiles led to a network of plowed roads, which bison also began using to move freely beyond their winter range in the park. The "cost" of winter living went down, and the buffalo population in the park grew, as did human confrontations with bison. In addition, area ranchers became concerned by a perceived threat of spreading the brucellosis strain carried by the Yellowstone bison herd. (Photo © Layne Kennedy)

World's largest buffalo

The world's largest buffalo is "a concrete replica of the beasts which once thundered across the plains," according to the chamber of commerce in Jamestown, North Dakota, where this symbolic statue stands. Some fifty feet (15 m) high, the roadside attraction neighbors Jamestown's Old Frontier Town and can be seen by passing travelers on Interstate 94. (Photo © Layne Kennedy)

Buffalo and wolf pack
Early European explorers in North America saw not only large bison herds but also large wolf packs. Numerous explorers described the severe predation of wolves on bison; one such scene was immortalized by George Catlin in his early 1800s sketch of a bison protecting itself from a pack of marauding white wolves. The post-Columbian abundance of bison in North America, however, was almost certainly due to the decimation of a large portion of the Native North Americans' population by Eurasian diseases that decreased human hunting of bison and allowed herds to flourish.

try based on raising wild game is developing. Wildlife creates more than just material wealth and recreational satisfaction, however. To native people, wild animals are carriers of ancient traditions that would wither and die without them; others find wildlife an antidote to the siren call of urban life. We all are richer for the continued presence of wildlife in wild lands around us.

The buffalo stands for a system of wildlife conservation in North America that is the most successful in the world. At the turn of the century, wildlife destruction was reversed, international wildlife conservation treaties were signed, the new profession of wildlife management came into being, and a well-thought-out system of protected areas arose in the form of national, provincial, and state parks, wildlife refuges, ecological reserves, and wildlife sanctuaries. The public banded together in thousands of small conservation organizations to save wildlife. Out of these small seeds grew large organizations such as the National Wildlife Federation and Canadian Wildlife Federation, Audubon Society, Izaak Walton League of America, Rocky Mountain Elk Foundation, and others. The American Bison Society, its task essentially completed, took the proud step in 1935 to vote itself out of existence.

Despite these past successes, what I saw that memorable day in Wood Buffalo National Park would, unfortunately, not last forever. The bison we saw were actually in rapid decline, and well-meaning actions taken on behalf of bison decades earlier were reaping bitter consequences. Concerns about disease and hybridization had led the agencies in charge of protecting bison in Canada to announce their intention of eliminating these buffalo—and with them the most important gene pool of the species *Bison bison*. To their credit, the agencies pulled back when public hearings exposed flaws in their kill-and-replace plan—including poor government conservation policies, as well as some science that we cannot be proud of. In short, the public hearings did exactly what they are intended to do. The remorseless workings of an industrial society such as ours will continually imperil conservation successes of the past. Relentless public vigilance is needed—even if bureaucracies exist for conservation—lest what has been achieved is inadvertently lost.

Yet, what shall we defend? The call to preserve wilderness has virtually universal political appeal, yet it is far from clear what "wilderness" we should preserve. The Earth we wish to preserve is in a constant state of change, and humans have played their part in this change for millennia. Take, for example, Yellowstone National Park, the first national park in the United States. It seems that Yellowstone cannot drop out of the national headlines, be it over the plight of its grizzly bears—an epic saga in itself forest fires, poaching by criminals masquerading as hunters, or the growth of elk herds.

Should park management exercise a hands-off approach to management with modest attempts to complete the ecosystem deficits? Or should park management exercise a hands-on approach to create ecosystems as they were a century and a half ago, when ungulate numbers were low because of constant predation by native people and the woody vegetation was richer because grazing levels were correspondingly lower? The proponents of the first view argue that the high number of ungulates in the park today reflects conditions as they were before Europeans arrived on the continent. The other side argues that pre-contact conditions were based on a much richer vegetation and a scarcity of large herbivores and carnivores. What should be the benchmark for management today?

The "pre-contact days" philosophy promotes North America before Christopher Columbus's 1492 arrival in the New World as though it were the natural state of the continent. We should be aware, however, that North America at the time Columbus landed was not the natural wilderness it was seen to be by the newly arrived Europeans. What the native peoples did to North America before the arrival of Columbus was no more "natural" than what early Europeans did to Europe, and the wildlife that existed on this continent before the arrival of the native peoples was different from the wildlife Europeans found in the seventeenth and eighteenth centuries.

North America, its landscape, and the animals that live in it have undergone, and continue to undergo, tremendous change. The challenge for the future of our planet will be our ability to manage this change.

▲▲▲ Chapter 1 ▲▲▲

ORIGINS OF THE BUFFALO

The buffalo represents the people and the universe and should always be treated with respect, for was he not here before the two-legged peoples, and is he not generous in that he gives us our homes and our food? The buffalo is wise in many things, and, thus, we should learn from him and should always be as a relative with him.

—Oglala Sioux holy man Black Elk,
describing the Sun Dance, *The Sacred Pipe*, 1953

I KNOW A HILL IN THE PRAIRIE, A HILL FULL OF LIFE. I ROAMED OVER IT MANY times as a high school student, scouting for treasures. Low aspen bluffs flanked its western slope, and chokecherries and saskatoon berries grew on top. Late spring and summer brought a profusion of wildflowers to its slopes. Below, there were small meadows with native prairie, knee-high thickets of prickly prairie rose, and dense snowberry bushes. Wolf willow greeted summer with an overpowering scent. Crows and magpies nested here, meadowlarks sang from fenceposts, Savannah sparrows chirped from tangles of wheat grass, northern shrike balanced on barbed-wire fences, and red-tailed hawks soared overhead. Once, in early winter, I stood in awe as a huge flock of sharp-tailed grouse flew overhead—the largest flock I have ever seen. Here I heard the plaintive cry of a newborn porcupine and in the evening the howling of coyotes. Here I shot my first snowshoe hare and not far away my first whitetail buck, a fine five-pointer. I grew up thinking of the prairie as a landscape rich in life.

But I had been deceived.

I accepted the prairie as I found it, happy for every square foot not plowed under or overgrazed by livestock. I had not seen the prairie during its modern heyday. George Catlin's *Letters and Notes on the North American Indians* of 1841, Francis Parkman's accounts of his 1845 travels in *The Oregon Trail*, or Major William Francis Butler's narrative of his travels across the Canadian plains in the mid-1800s all hint at what it must have been like: herds of mustangs, pronghorns, and elk; clouds of waterfowl; and huge buffalo herds followed by large packs of white wolves that looked as though they were flocks of sheep. Wolf packs of seventy plus are beyond our imagination; wolf poisoners occasionally killed that many at a single poisoned carcass. It is hard to imagine meeting hundreds of grizzly bears, yet that is what explorer O. G. Pattie saw in 1831 along the Arkansas River. He counted 220 in one day, eight of which were killed by his party when the bears attacked.

I believed the prairie of a century or two ago was rich in species. That, too, was an error, for the prairie was low in species even when Christopher Columbus arrived in the New World in 1492. The species-rich fauna that evolved on this continent for millions of years and over successive cycles of continental glaciations went largely extinct at the end of the Ice Age some 10,000 years ago. That was North America's "natural fauna," and it is no more. It is today known as the Rancholabrean fauna, after the bone deposits found in the tar pits of Rancho La Brea in Los Angeles.

Life in the Ice Age

In Ice Age North America, the plains teemed with horses and camels, huge Colombian mammoths with long, curving tusks, and peccaries nearly as large as wild boar. Mastodons as tall as Indian elephants but bulkier lived in the coniferous forests. Ground sloths—some as large as an elephant, the smallest the size of a grizzly, and all well armed and armored against predator attacks—stripped trees of bark and branches for their food. Tiny pronghorns lived in prairie shrubs, and a larger four-horned version roamed the Rocky Mountain foothills. There were deer the size and shape of mountain goats, and big, long-legged, large-hoofed moose with huge ornate antlers. Whitetail deer were rare but wide ranging, as were blacktail deer along the Pacific coast. Mountain goats extended in range to central Mexico. Bighorn sheep were rare, but spread and became numerous late in the glaciation. There were *Euceratheres*—larger, big-horned relatives of the musk ox—in the Rockies. Herbivores in the north included caribou, Dall's sheep, Przewalski's horses, saiga antelope, yak, elk, woolly mammoths, and long-legged forest musk ox. Large-horned North American bison, veritable giants, were found on the Pacific coast as well as in the continent's interior.

BUFFALO AT ICY DAWN
Pages 16–17, main photo: *A young buffalo bull stands silhouetted on a ridge in Yellowstone National Park, backlit by the morning sun. (Photo © Jeff and Alexa Henry)*

BISON PETROGLYPH
Page 17, inset: *Chipped into the rock of a Utah canyon wall, this bison with two protruding arrows or spears is believed to date from the Fremont culture, 600 to 1250 A.D.*

And then there were predators—and what predators! There were true lions on the plains, like those in Africa, only larger. There were cheetahlike running cats closely related to, but larger than, puma. There were lion-sized saber-toothed cats with powerful, well-muscled forelimbs, which probably hunted in large packs. There were elegant scimitar cats, about as large as saber-toothed cats, but with longer legs and built more lightly for running. There were large jaguars and big packs of hyenalike dire wolves about as tall as gray wolves but more massively built. There were wolf-sized coyotes. Overhead circled huge condorlike vultures as well as hawks that are no longer with us. Black bears were present but were secretive and scarce. Gray wolves roamed Alaska and Yukon, and may have followed the glacial fronts to the south of the continent; however, their remains are scarce. The largest predator was the huge carnivorous short-faced bear or "bull-dog bear," *Arctodus simus*, which exceeded all living bears in size.

The teeth of Rancholabrean predators were badly worn compared to those of modern predators, suggesting a tough life for predators in Pleistocene North America. Tooth fractures in dire wolves, coyotes, saber-toothed cats, and lions recovered from the Rancho La Brea tar pits are three times larger than those of modern carnivores. It seems these ancient predators hunted prey that worked hard to escape.

The unusual animals that lived in North America also had a marked influence on the vegetation and landscape. Colombian mammoth, mastodons, and ground sloths trampled trees as they stripped the leaves and bark for food, creating a rich underbrush interspersed with the occasional massive old-growth tree that escaped the browsing. Grazing by mammoth, bison, and horses removed mature grass in fertile areas. Reduced grass cover and discontinuous forest canopies meant that forest and prairie fires were rare and relatively small.

Ancestors of the Bison

Like all cattle, the bison's earliest ancestors were tropical and subtropical species in the extreme south of Asia millions of years before the Ice Age. Unlike other cattle, bison colonized open grasslands early in their history, first in temperate and then in cold climates. We know little of this early history, which began 4 million years ago and terminated with the beginning of the major glaciations about 1.7 million years ago. These early bison were relatively small, short horned, and fleet of foot. With the onset of the Ice Age, a northern plains bison, the steppe wisent, evolved in Eurasia and colonized the nutrient-rich, fertile ecosystems that formed under the influence of continental and alpine glaciers.

During glacial ages, loess steppe, glaciers, glacial moraines, and huge glacial lakes dominated the landscape; collectively, these features are known as the "mammoth steppe." In the Ice Age, the mammoth steppe extended from eastern Siberia into Alaska and Yukon, allowing animals to roam between North America and Siberia.

One species that entered southern North America about 300,000 years ago and survived to become a characteristic species of its fauna was the Eurasian steppe bison, *Bison priscus*. The precise external appearance of early *Bison priscus* is not know, but those recorded in cave paint-

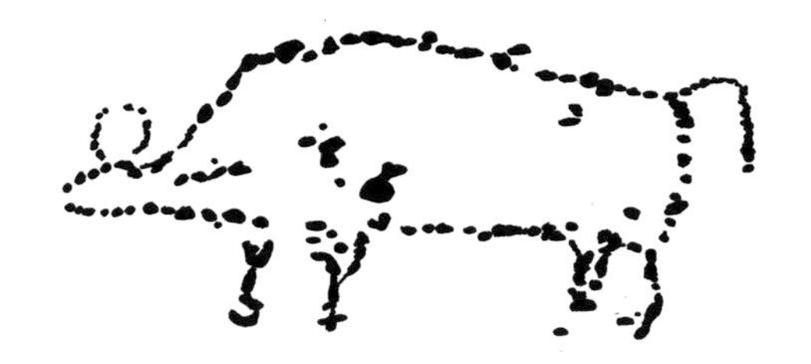

BUFFALO BOULDER EFFIGY
A rendering of a large effigy of a buffalo as seen from the air. The sculpture is of unknown origin and is believed to date from the pre-contact era. It is made of glacial boulders arranged on the prairie near Big Beaver, Saskatchewan.

ings of the Upper Paleolithic Era had long, graceful horns and an ornate hair coat different from modern bison.

Three vital security adaptations shaped *Bison priscus* before it arrived in North America: life in the herd, outrunning predators, and, where feasible, confronting and deterring predators. Bison, like many large ungulates living on open plains, opted for life in the "selfish herd." Security is the top priority for living beings—all else is secondary—so joining into groups has advantages. Some people believe that the advantage of herds is that they provide more pairs of eyes to spot predators earlier than one pair, but this is not the sole reason as herds still form at night when unseen predators are most active. Moreover, the herd produces a lot of noise and scent, making it difficult to detect predators.

The most important advantage of a herd is safety in numbers, also known as the *dilution effect*. In a herd, the attention of predators is not focused on any one in-

BUFFALO STAMPEDE
A herd of bison charge down a grassy hill in Yellowstone National Park, presenting a formidable defense against predators. With its horns and powerful legs, as well as its herd lifestyle, the modern bison retains security adaptations of its ancestral Asian bison species: the ability to outrun or confront predators. The most important advantage of living in a herd is protection, providing safety in numbers. (Photo © Erwin and Peggy Bauer)

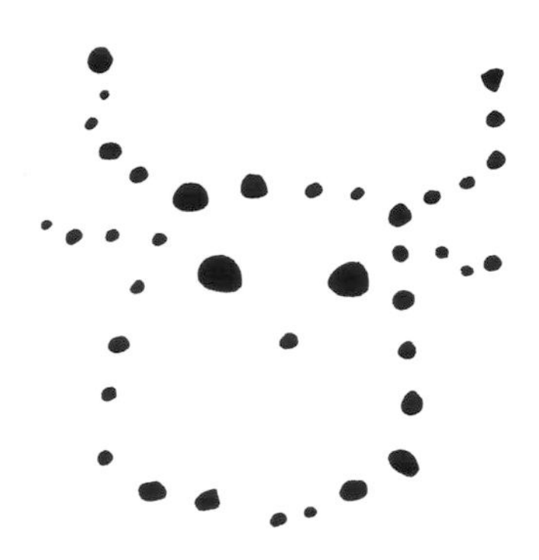

BUFFALO FACE PETROGLYPH
This visage of a bison is of unknown origin and is believed to date from the pre-contact era. It is made up of small holes pecked and drilled into a rock outcropping at Roche Percee, Saskatchewan.

dividual but is diluted among the many. Hence, the larger the herd, the better.

The most important requirement for life in the herd is getting along with others of one's own kind so as to neither injure nor alienate them. Aggressive individuals who injure others place themselves in jeopardy as the injured attract predators. Consequently, herd species evolve without the weapons of combat that maximize surface damage in combatants and that are typical of territorial species. Instead, individuals develop large complex horns, antlers, and tusks to catch opponents' charges and to lock heads during full-strength engagements. Now sporting-type wrestling becomes feasible and sparring is practiced by young and old males outside the mating season.

Despite the security afforded by the herd, life on the open plains required evading fleet-footed predators. As there is little or no opportunity to hide, the only option is rapid, sustained flight so that the prey may leave the predator behind and lose itself in the vastness of space. Speedy, long-distance running requires large organs for blood circulation and gas exchange. Thus, Eurasian northern plains bison, exposed to wolves and running cats, evolved into large-bodied runners.

Bison also developed a style of running. For sustained flight from predators, runners—or cursors—keep their body level and lift their legs as little as possible to save energy for endurance. In contrast, saltors, such as deer, lift their body high during each jump and soon tire. Saltors run so as to hide quickly in cover, so they need not run far; this option is not available on the open plains. Saltors have large, muscular hind quarters and small front quarters, and their hind legs are longer than the front legs. Cursors have well-developed, muscular front quarters and small hind quarters; their legs are fairly light-boned so they cost little to lift, and their hind and front legs are of similar length. A bison's hump allows it to extend its stride with the front legs, and the longer the stride, the faster the bison. When it runs, the bison shifts much of the power from the hind legs to the front legs, and the hind legs deliver just enough power to maintain propulsion. The fast-moving plains bison that were later hunted by the native peoples were a challenge to any horse; few horses could run down more than one buffalo in a hunt. A "three-buffalo horse" was a treasure to the Native North American hunter.

Bison priscus not only ran away from predators, but also, when it was advantageous, turned on bears and large cats attacking singly or in small groups. It used social defense formations in which members of the same herd assisted one another when confronting predators, as shown by archaeological excavations of human kill sites suggesting that the bison were making a musk-ox–like stand. The long horns of the Eurasian steppe bison had outward-pointing tips similar to the horn tips of cape buffalo and musk ox, two species that regularly take on predators.

The Advent of a Giant Bison

Bison priscus was not small when it crossed from Siberia, but under severe predation pressure in North America, it grew relatively quickly into the gigantic *Bison latifrons* with even larger horns and a higher hump. Compared to its smaller descendent, *Bison bison*, it also developed legs that favored speed over power.

Large body size is not only an aid in

▲▲▲ Native North American Legends ▲▲▲

The Wellspring of Buffalo

Many Native North Americans came to rely on the buffalo for food as well as clothing, shelter, and as a source for myriad daily utensils, toys, and more. As Oglala Sioux Chief Red Cloud told a white man in tallying the twenty-two uses the Native North Americans had for the bison, "His meat sustained life." It was little wonder that the buffalo also became a focus for the spiritual life of many Native North Americans, and the stories of the creation of buffalo were important legends, often helping explain the origin of human beings as well.

A recurring theme in buffalo creation stories of the plains Indians centers on a cave or hole in the earth from which the bison came forth like a spring of water. Crow Chief Plenty-coups told his biographer Frank Bird Linderman of his vision of this source of the buffalo in the Crazy Mountains of Montana, recounted in *American: The Life Story of a Great Indian, Plenty-coups, Chief of the Crows* (The John Day Company, Inc., 1930):

. . . FROM THE PEAK in the Crazy Mountains I saw a Buffalo-bull. . . . I got up and started to go to the Bull, because I knew he was the Person who wanted me. . . .

Then he shook his red rattle and sang a queer song four times. "Look!" he pointed.

Out of the hole in the ground came the buffalo, bulls and cows and calves without number. They spread wide and blackened the plains. Everywhere I looked great herds of buffalo were going in every direction, and still others without number were pouring out of the hole in the ground to travel on the wide plains.

Folklorist Katharine Berry Judson also recorded this Teton Sioux story in *Myths and Legends of the Great Plains* (A. C. McClurg & Co., 1913):

IN THE DAYS of the grandfathers, buffaloes lived under the earth. In the olden times, they say, a man who was journeying came to a hill where there were many holes in the ground. He entered one of them. When he had gone inside he found buffalo chips and buffalo tracks on all sides. He found also buffalo hairs where the buffaloes had rubbed against the walls. These were the real buffaloes and they lived under the ground. Afterwards some of them came to the surface of the earth and lived there. Then the herds on the earth increased.

Explorer Colonel Richard Irving Dodge met other plains Indians who said they knew of the underground wellspring of bison, some stating that the source was a huge cave in northwest Texas. As Dodge recounted in his 1883 book, *Our Wild Indians*:

ONE INDIAN HAS gravely and solemnly assured me that he has been at these caverns, and with his own eyes saw the buffalo coming out in countless throngs. Others have told me that their fathers or uncles, or some other of the old men have been there. In 1879 Stone Calf assured me that he knew exactly where these caves were, though he had never seen them, that the Good God had provided this means for the constant supply of food for the Indian, and that however recklessly the white men might slaughter, they never could exterminate them. When last I saw him, the old man was beginning to waiver in this belief, and feared that the Bad God had shut up the openings and that his people might starve.

BISON PRISCUS
The long-horned Bison priscus *was the Eurasian and Alaskan steppe wisent that crossed from Siberia into Alaska during the Ice Age. This drawing was reconstructed based on cave art and was confirmed by scientist Dale Guthrie based on a* Bison priscus *mummy found preserved in the Alaskan permafrost. (Drawing by Valerius Geist)*

BISON LATIFRONS/BISON ANTIQUUS
The giant Bison latifrons *had a high hump and was geared for running from predators.* Bison latifrons *existed in North America for some 300,000 years, dying out about 22,000 years ago. It was succeeded by the smaller-bodied* Bison antiquus, *which died out about 10,000 years ago.* Bison antiquus *was the source of the Folsom bison-hunting culture of 11,000 to 10,000 B.P. (Drawing by Valerius Geist)*

BISON BISON
Today's North American Bison bison *is but a shy dwarf compared to the monstrous bison of the North American Pleistocene epoch of some one million years ago. The dwarfing of body and horn size following the Ice Age can be attributed to the impact of human hunters—namely the selective killing of large, bold bison that readily confronted humans. (Drawing by Valerius Geist)*

sustained running, it is also an asset when confronting large predators. But why larger—even gigantic—horns in response to predation? To better defend oneself against attacking predators? Not at all. The logic of larger horns in response to severe predation runs differently. To a plains-dwelling ungulate, high speed and endurance are essential to escape from predators. Thus, the newborn calf is in a perilous condition, and ideally it would be as fast and enduring as its mother. Consequently, the more highly developed the young must be at birth. Therefore, the birth-weight must go up, and the fat, protein, and sugar content of the mother's milk should also increase.

In order to produce large, developed young and rich milk, the female must have superior capacities to spare resources for reproduction from her own living requirements. The female should be searching for a mate that is at least her equal, but preferably her superior, in resources. The male can signal its superiority by growing "luxury organs" that are costly in material resources, such as horns, antlers, and nuptial hair coats. These organs must be sensitive to environmental quality, enlarging when conditions are good and shrinking when they are not. Bison males with large horns signal that they are so good at procuring and processing forage that they have plenty of nutrients and energy to spare. Consequently, the most "attractive" bull is the one with the largest horns and the most ornate body. Thus, the dramatic increase in bison's horn size after their mid-Pleistocene entry into North America is to be expected.

Bison latifrons, the giant bison with its immense sweep of horns, characterized North America's Rancholabrean fauna for nearly 300,000 years. After its sudden ap-

▲▲▲ Native North American Legends ▲▲▲

Creator Sun Makes the Buffalo From Mud

At seventy years of age in 1985, Percy Bullchild, a Blackfeet from Montana, published a collection of stories entitled *The Sun Came Down: The History of the World as My Blackfeet Elders Told It*. Among these stories is a Blackfeet version of the creation of the buffalo, made from mud by the Sun:

CREATOR SUN TOOK some of the mud again, as he had done when he made Mudman. And with his hands he molded a thing with four legs on it, a head and the body. The Mudman was astounded at his father's making. After this thing was shaped by Creator Sun's skilled hands, he made the thing's nostrils and held it up to his mouth. He blew very hard into this thing's nostrils. Creator Sun, as he blew into the thing, said to it, "Now breathe the air from me, my breath, and live with it like my children are now living with it. Eat the food of grass and foliage to fatten you and those in the same likeness as you are that will all roam this land sometime soon. Abound this land and become the food for my children." As this new thing came to life from that blow into its nostrils, it got up on its feet, and it too was very wobbly on the legs as it tried to walk away from them. This new thing fell back down but kept on trying to stand up and walk. . . . This was the first flesh food given to the Mudman and all of their children to supplement those roots, berries, and the barks of food, which they ate for a very long time. This particular creature . . . became the food animal known as the buffalo.

pearance, it changed gradually to a smaller-bodied and smaller-horned form that varied regionally and fluctuated in size over time. Several forces were at work in the reshaping of the giant bison into the smaller—but still large—*Bison antiquus*.

A species of animals is expected to be large when they are colonizing a new area, scientists believe. Because there are relatively few individuals and there is plenty of food to go around, colonizers can indulge in luxurious body growth. This is known as the *dispersal* form of a species. Severe predation pressure selects for dispersal-type individuals by insuring low densities of a prey species. A high predation level also prolongs the time when dispersal-type individuals characterize the species. Consequently, if the Eurasian steppe bison, *Bison priscus*, enters into an environment with severe predation pressure in North America, its dispersal descendant, *Bison latifrons*, is expected to remain as such for a long time—and so it did. *Latifrons*-type bison remained for a long time in the extreme North American west, while in the center of the continent the bison shrank to the dimensions of *Bison antiquus*. The last *Bison latifrons* populations died out about 22,000 years ago. Thereafter, bison of *Bison antiquus* dimensions were left behind, surviving until about 10,000 B.P. (Before Present time).

When habitats are filled to capacity and populations must compete with other species and among themselves for high-quality food, we expect a small-bodied *maintenance* form. After the colonization period there begins a new form of evolution called *efficiency selection*: When high-quality resources essential for reproduction become scarce, individuals who can do more with less win the reproductive game The more efficient individuals are in reducing the costs of daily maintenance and growth, the more resources they can spare for reproduction.

Yet throughout these modest size fluctuations, the North American long-horned bison remained much the same animal. It wasn't until the arrival of human hunters at the end of the Ice Age that the bison underwent further dramatic changes.

▲▲▲ Native North American Legends ▲▲▲

Buffalo Woman Leads the Buffalo Out of the Earth

Western historian Mari Sandoz recounted a Pawnee telling the story of the beginning of the world in her book *The Buffalo Hunters* (Hastings House, 1954). This legend has as its central characters both the buffalo and a mother figure, Buffalo Woman; Sandoz recounts that many plains Indian stories describe a mother figure with the wisdom of the buffalo:

ONCE, LONG AGO, all things were waiting in a deep place far underground. There were the great herds of buffaloes and all the people, and the antelope too, and wolves, deer and rabbits—everything, even the little bird that sings the *tear-tear* song. Everything waited as in sleep.

Then the one called Buffalo Woman awoke, stretched her arms, rose and began to walk. She walked among all the creatures, past the little *tear-tear* bird, the rabbits and all the rest and through the people too, and the buffaloes. Everywhere as she passed there was an awakening, and a slow moving, as when the eyes were making ready for some fine new thing to be seen.

Buffalo Woman walked on in the good way, past even the farthest buffaloes, the young cows with their sleeping yellow calves. She went on to a dark round place that seemed like a hole and she stood there a while, looking. Then she bowed her head a little as one does to pass under the lodge flap, and stepped out. Suddenly the people could see there was a great shining light all about her, a shining and brightness that seemed blinding as she was gone.

And now a young cow arose and followed the woman, and then another buffalo and another, until a great string of them was following, each one for a moment in the shining light of the hole before he was gone, and the light fell upon the one behind.

When the last of the buffaloes was up and moving, the people began to rise, one after another, and fell into a row too, each one close upon the heels of the moccasins ahead. All the people, young and old and weak and strong went so, out through the hole that was on Pahuk, out upon the shining, warm and grassy place that was the earth, with a wide river, the Platte, flowing below, and over everything a blueness, with the *tear-tear* bird flying toward the sun, the warming sun.

The buffaloes were already scattering over the prairie, feeding, spreading in every direction toward the circle that is the horizon. The people looked all around and knew this was their place, the place upon which they would live forever, they and the buffalo together.

The End of the Ice Age

Humans owe their ability to live in cold climates to the evolution of Ice Age mammals, which store up to 20 to 25 percent of their body mass as fat. Humans cannot live on lean meat alone (in fact, that is so debilitating a diet it is virtually fatal). We can, however, live on lean meat if we also eat either sufficient carbohydrates or fat. In hunter-gatherer or agricultural cultures, plants are a source of carbohydrates; in cold climates, plant food plays a subordinate role and fat takes the place of carbohydrates.

The Rancholabrean fauna successfully resisted the entry of humans for tens of thousands of years. Human hunters not only found prey difficult to hunt but had difficulty defending themselves against huge, hungry predators, and plant food was limited by the presence of highly specialized herbivores. As the Laurentide ice sheaths became thinner with the melting glaciers, cold Arctic air spilled south into mid-latitude North America, having devastating consequences on flora and fauna.

Buffalo pictograph
An image of a bison painted on a rock face in the Pryor Mountains of Montana. (Photo © Michael H. Francis)

Indeed, it may have led to the extinction of the North American cheetah and the disappearance of the giant bear, *Arctodus*, during the severe cold pulses of the Older Dryas glacial advance 13,000 years ago. With the extinction of the fearsome *Arctodus*, Paleo-Indians could finally hunt in relative safety and retain their kills. Megaherbivore populations, released from severe predation and aided by a warm phase in the climate, rebounded forcefully. About 12,500 years ago, people entered Alaska, and around 11,600 years ago, the Clovis elephant hunters roamed over mid-latitude North America.

The Clovis elephant hunters specialized in hunting Colombian mammoths and, in a few centuries, exterminated them. There followed the Folsom bison-hunting culture from about 11,000 to 10,000 B.P., which focused on the indigenous Rancholabrean bison, *Bison antiquus*. Both Paleo-Indian cultures used thick, sturdy spear points, suggesting a hand-held spear requiring that hunters engage prey from short distances. Despite an abundance of potential prey species, Paleo-Indian hunters killed almost exclusively Colombian mammoth and *Bison antiquus*, suggesting the perfection of a

The White Buffalo Woman

For it was the White Buffalo Cow Women who, in the beginning, brought to us our most sacred pipe, and from that time we have been relatives with the four-leggeds and all that moves. Tatanka, *the buffalo, is the closest four-legged relative that we have, and they live as a people, as we do.*
—Black Elk, *The Sacred Pipe*, 1953

The story of the White Buffalo Woman's coming to the Lakota is a powerful legend on many levels. It tells of the origin of many Lakota traditions and of the people's finding their place in the order of the world.

The legend also tells of the origin of the calumet, the ceremonial pipe that remains the Lakota's "most sacred heirloom," as John (Fire) Lame Deer wrote in *Lame Deer Seeker of Visions*: "Nothing of importance, good or bad, takes place among us without the pipe."

Finally, the story is a prophecy, telling of the sacred white buffalo that will come one day to unite all races to live together in harmony.

This narrative has been told and retold throughout time by spiritual leaders from Black Elk to Lame Deer. The version as paraphrased here was told by Lone Man and recorded by Frances Densmore in *Teton Sioux Music* (Bureau of American Ethnology, 1918).

One summer long ago the Sans-Arc (Without Bows) band of Lakota started toward the west seeking buffalo and other game to store for their winter supply. They searched everywhere but there was no game and the people were starving. A council was called and two young men were chosen to go off in quest of buffalo.

Coming to the crest of a hill, the young hunters saw in the west a solitary object advancing toward them. It did not look like a buffalo; it looked more like a human being. As it came nearer, they saw that it was a beautiful young maiden, more beautiful than any they could ever imagine, wearing a white buckskin dress, leggings, and moccasins. Her hair was hanging loose, except at the left side, where a tuft of buffalo hair was tied. In her right hand she carried a fan made of sage. Her face was painted with red vertical stripes. From her beauty and the way she floated instead of walking, the young men realized she was *wakan*, holy.

One of the hunters saw her beauty and had impure thoughts, desiring her. Suddenly a cloud came down and enveloped this young man. When the cloud left the earth the young man was left there—only a skeleton.

She spoke, thus: "Good news I am bringing, something holy to your Nation. A message I carry for your people from the Buffalo Nation.

"Go home and tell the chief to put up a special lodge in the middle of the camp circle. Let them spread sage at the place of honor. I have something of importance to present to the tribe, which will have a great deal to do with their future welfare. I shall be in the camp about sunrise."

The holy maiden commanded the pure scout to return to camp to do her wishes.

Early the next morning at daybreak, men, women, and children assembled around the special lodge in the camp to wait for the holy maiden. She appeared and walked slowly into the camp carrying a pipe. The chief brought the maiden to the lodge and made her a gift of rainwater in a buffalo horn, which was all the food they had to give.

The maiden arose, took up the pipe, and said:

"My relatives, brothers and sisters: I represent the Buffalo Nation, who has sent you this pipe. This pipe shall be used as a peacemaker." And she taught the people how to use the pipe and ceremonies for lighting it, saying that the smoke rising from the pipe was the breath of the Great Mystery Spirit, *Wakan Tanka*.

She then spoke to the women and told them that their gift given to them by *Wakan Tanka* of kindness toward every living creature would sustain the people. She gave them further gifts of corn and pemmican, and taught them how to make fire.

She spoke to the children and told them they were the coming generation and must learn how to use the pipe.

She spoke to the men and said: "In giving you this pipe you are expected to use it for nothing but good purposes. The tribe as a whole shall depend upon it for their needs. You realize that

Blackfoot calumet and pipe
This pipe bowl was carved from red catlinite, or pipestone, from the sacred Pipestone quarry in Minnesota, and is adorned with a realistically carved image of a buffalo. The calumet was crafted in the 1950s and belonged to Canadian Blackfoot Chief Ben Calf Robe. (Artifact #H77.94.3a; Ethnology Program, Provincial Museum of Alberta, Edmonton, Canada)

all your necessities of life come from the earth below, sky above, and four winds. You should revere them. When you are in need of buffalo meat, smoke this pipe and ask for what you need and it shall be granted you."

Then she lit the sacred pipe with a buffalo chip. She said, "I offer this to *Wakan Tanka* for all the good that comes from above. I offer this to the earth, whence come all good gifts. I offer this to the four winds, whence come all good things."

Rising, she left the lodge and walked away. As the people watched, she stopped and rolled over four times. The first time she turned into a black buffalo, then a brown one, then a red one. Finally she turned into a white buffalo and was gone.

White buffalo bull
Big Medicine was a famous large albino bull who lived in the National Bison Range, Montana. He was born in captivity in 1933 and lived for twenty-six years before dying in 1959. Big Medicine, now stuffed and mounted, currently stands in the Montana State Historical Society Museum in Helena. (Photo © Erwin and Peggy Bauer)

I bought a beautiful white buffalo skin from Le Cèdre, who had killed the young bull last January at Grandes Fourches; the hair was long, soft, and perfectly white, resembling a sheep's fleece. . . .They have a superstition that many superior virtues are contained in a skin of this kind, and imagine it to be the most essential article an Indian can possess.
—Alexander Henry the Younger, Northwest Company fur trader, Journals, *April 25, 1803*

BISON PRISCUS CAVE PAINTING
This steppe wisent image appears on a wall in the vast network of caves at Niaux, France, many of which are covered by prehistoric cave paintings.

hunting style in which mammoth and bison were made to stand and face hunters.

The Achilles heel of large mammals that human hunters have exploited since antiquity is their tendency to defend their young by confronting, attacking, and chasing off predators. Once Folsom hunters learned how to evade an attack, they could reliably kill by goading a predictable, pugnacious *Bison antiquus* into a confrontation. Folsom kill sites contain one or two bison, quite unlike mass kill sites of a later age, suggesting that bison in the Folsom age stood to face predators much as musk ox do. While bison today do not stand like musk ox, they show vestiges of this behavior as they form "loose stands" against single or paired wolves, and sometimes turn and confront human hunters.

The warm climate declined into another severe cold phase lasting from about 11,000 to 10,000 B.P. During this time, the remaining Rancholabrean fauna probably shrank in species number and population and was displaced south and to lower elevations. East Siberian mammals entered the south, and foremost among the newcomers was *Bison occidentalis*. This smaller, cold-adapted bison replaced the southern *Bison antiquus* at mid-latitudes abruptly about 10,000 B.P. The Eurasian bison was probably more resistant to human hunting than *Bison antiquus* due to its long evolutionary history in contact with humans in Asia. This influence began first with bison in Beringia, of which Alaska is the eastern extension. Here *Bison priscus* and the later *Bison occidentalis* encountered hunters, who, towards the end of the Pleistocene, appear to have used hand-thrown light spears tipped with bone points that had microblades embedded in their sides. This indicates that the Beringian bison of 12,000 to 11,000 B.P. would not stand and confront human hunters. *Bison occidentalis* shrank in body size under the influence of such hunting before it appeared in mid-latitude North America to replace *Bison antiquus*. Consequently, because *Bison occidentalis* could probably not be approached as closely as the larger *Bison antiquus*, the Folsom culture came to an end. The stabbing spear was replaced by a throwing spear and a new means of hunting bison.

The Changing Bison

The reduction in bison numbers and distribution after 11,000 B.P. was probably at the expense of *Bison antiquus*, and the subsequent recovery in numbers and range due to *Bison occidentalis*. These two bison species likely hybridized during the long warm phase beginning 10,000 B.P. The bison survived, but it was no longer the old bison. The giant, large-headed, long-horned bison became a small-headed, short-horned "dwarf." Moreover, the small bison's teeth changed as it became an efficient grazer, and its body form changed so that it was no longer a superlative high-speed runner.

By about 5,000 B.P., bison had reached the size of the present-day northern or wood bison, shrinking in body size even further in the south. The size of the bison's skeleton shrunk by about 10 percent, indicating a reduction in sheer mass of about 30 percent. The reduction in skull and horn dimensions was even greater and more dramatic. All this occurred in only a few thousand years. What happened?

The bison's environment changed, but it had changed before without the bison becoming a short-horned dwarf. An analysis by scientist Dale Guthrie in his book

HOWLING WOLF

Alongside humans, gray wolves have been the principle predators of bison. Thus, through time, buffalo have adapted to protect themselves against wolves, favoring their ability to run from a marauding wolf and the need for front-facing horns to confront and deter a wolf's attack. (Photo © Gerry Ellis/ Ellis Nature Photography)

noth Steppe sug-
ody form follow-
volutionary re-
change in the
on after the end

istocene history,
th America were
mbush predators
ed cats, and large
ulling predators
ey, such as gray
on's response to the cats and bears hunting alone or in small numbers was to confront and attack as well as to form defensive formations to protect their own thin-skinned flanks and hindquarters. This requires large bodies and sweeping horns that may be used to hook and wound a predator or to block its way to the vulnerable rear. It also requires a keen attraction to the bawling of calves in danger and a pugnacious disposition. The response to culling predators such as wolves, however, was flight. If wolves attack in a pack, it is impossible for bison

▲▲▲ Native North American Legends ▲▲▲

The Buffalo Being Attacks

Legends still remain of giant buffaloes attacking people, legends handed down from prehistory by word of mouth. This Teton Sioux story was recorded by Katharine Berry Judson in *Myths and Legends of the Great Plains* (A. C. McClurg & Co., 1913):

ONCE UPON A time, a Buffalo Being attacked a party of Indians. He killed one of them, but the others ran away and climbed a tree. The Buffalo Being followed them and rushed at the tree. He rushed many times, knocking off piece after piece of the tree, until very little was left.

Then the frightened Indians lighted some tinder, and threw it far off into the tall grass. The fire scorched the Buffalo Being's eyes, and injured his horns. The hard part of the horn slipped off, leaving only the softer part, so that he could no longer injure any one.

But the Buffalo Being was still dangerous. At last one of the Indians slipped down the tree, with his bow and arrow. He killed the Buffalo Being. Then all the men came down the tree and skinned the animal and cut up the flesh. Into the buffalo-skin robe they placed the body of the dead Indian.

But suddenly another Buffalo Being appeared. The Indians again climbed the tree. But this Being only walked four times around the dead Indian. Then he said, "Arise to your feet."

At once the dead man came to life. The Buffalo Being said to him, "Hereafter you shall be mysterious. The sun, the moons, the four winds, day and night shall be your slaves."

Then it was so. The Indian could take the form of a fine plume, which was blown against a tree. It would stick to the tree and wave many times in the breeze.

standing their ground to protect their flanks, belly, testes, and haunches. The long-horned bison in Eurasia's mammoth steppe and in the North American Rancholabrean had to be masters of *both* confrontational defense and enduring flight. By the end of the Ice Age, bison no longer faced large cats and predacious bears; the major predator was now pack-hunting gray wolves. The bison's willingness to confront wolves was now counteradaptive; the best security strategy was to run. Consequently, small-horned, small-bodied bison evolved.

Guthrie's argument is an important beginning, but it needs to be extended when we consider that modern bison, compared with long-horned bison, are geared for power rather than speed.

Compared with their Rancholabrean counterparts, the dire wolves, gray wolves were not fast, but they were nevertheless enduring runners of great persistence and thus supremely effective predators. Consequently, bison relied not on speed but on endurance to tire wolves by running over ground sharply varying in elevation and covered with low obstacles that hin-

BUFFALO AT SUNSET
Pages 32–33: *A bison herd grazes on a ridge against the setting sun in Wyoming. The daily life of grazers such as bison requires long periods of undisturbed grazing. Fibrous plant matter is difficult to digest, and grazers live on a slim margin of surplus energy at the best of times. The margin of safety between success and starvation is narrow. (Photo © Jeff and Alexa Henry)*

dered wolves but not the larger bison.

Gray wolves are "snow dogs" that, for the greater part of the year, travel through snow on oversized paws. These paws allow for speedy swimming in a northern landscape that is seasonally rich in water. On soft ground, their paws also allow gray wolves to quickly overtake bison, whose relatively small hooves sink deep with every step. Choosing hard ground must, therefore, be important to bison for fast, secure flight and may be the reason bison form networks of trails. To outrun wolves, bison became geared for power rather than speed, and readily accepted gullies and badlands in their quest to escape.

Severe hunting pressure by Paleo-Indians also selected against bison that stood their ground and attacked predators. Bison that confronted hunters could be easily speared and killed; bison that fled would survive and thus have a reproductive advantage. The bison most likely to confront human hunters were the largest, strongest, healthiest, and thus most confident males. In spring and early summer, these bulls could have been enticed into attacking as they sought to protect calves, allowing human hunters an easy target for their spears. While female bison are lactating and depleted of fat in spring, bulls are laying down fat in preparation for the rutting season. To human hunters, bulls were then a source of vitally important fat that was scarce in late winter, spring, and early summer. Consequently, confrontational hunting killed off the largest, fattest, healthiest, bravest, and most aggressive bulls.

Without the need for large, fast runners, and therefore, without the need for large calves at birth, there was little selection by female bison for large-horned males. Instead, there would have been selection for bison who used their limited resources for reproduction. This would favor bison with smaller horns and heads.

Climatic changes also contributed to the bison's down-sizing. Drought cycles on the great plains were an important factor in periodically creating severe food shortages.

Compared with other wild cattle, modern bison are remarkably shy of humans and readily take flight, and there are no records of other cattle species being goaded into running over cliffs and abysses as were bison. Humans and gray wolves—together with periodic food shortages—had set the stage for efficiency selection to remove aggressive, long-horned bison. With *Bison occidentalis* began the age of human hunters driving shy bison into natural traps and, by 5,500 B.P., over cliffs.

Legends of Native North Americans recall this dramatic change. According to native tradition, the bison of the early days attacked and ate people. That changed when the people created bows and arrows; then the bison fled—but not before taking a mouthful of human flesh. To this day, this flesh may be viewed by skinning a bison's throat. There, right behind the jaws, one can see light-colored meat (the salivary glands)—the last bite of human flesh taken by the bison.

BUFFALO PICTOGRAPH WITH HUMAN INSIDE

Painted on a Dakota Winter Count chronicle of 1850 to 1851, these two pictographs depict bison with human figures inside of them. According to one of the artists, "a buffalo cow was killed . . . and an old woman found in her belly," as recounted by anthropologist Garrick Mallery in 1882 to 1883. Stories of bison swallowing human beings were perpetuated through time to become legend; the tales may have had their roots in early eras when monstrous bison were said to attack and eat people.

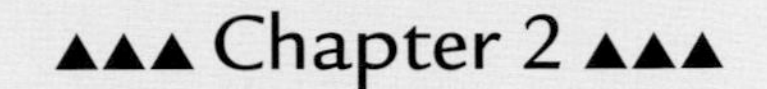

Chapter 2

The Hunter and the Hunted

The buffalo was part of us, his flesh and blood being absorbed by us until it became our own flesh and blood. Our clothing, our tipis, everything we needed for life came from the buffalo's body. It was hard to say where the animal ended and the man began.

—John (Fire) Lame Deer, *Lame Deer Seeker of Visions*, with Richard Erdoes, 1972

As North America's fauna evolved, so did human life styles. The large Rancholabrean carnivores and herbivores disappeared around 12,000 to 10,000 B.P., and were partially replaced by newly arrived Siberian immigrants, such as elk, moose, grizzly bears, bison, and humans. Corresponding with this change, some hunters on the great bison range diversified to become marginal hunter-gatherers while others became marginal agriculturists.

The shift in the hunters' lifestyle reflected a move from a time of affluence to a time of want. Their diet, previously dominated by meat and fat obtained reliably from large herbivores, now consisted mainly of plant food subsidized by animal meats low in fat, such as rabbits, rodents, small carnivores, fish,

His meat sustained life: it was cut in strips and dried, it was chopped up and packed in skins, its tallow and grease were preserved—all for winter use; its bones afforded material for implements and weapons; its skull was preserved as great medicine; its hide furnished blankets, garments, boats, ropes, and a warm and portable house; its hoofs produced glue, its sinews were used for bowstrings and a most excellent substitute for twine.

—Sioux Chief Red Cloud,
telling of the twenty-two uses for a buffalo

BUFFALO AT SUNRISE
Pages 36–37, main photo: *A herd of bison seek water along a stream at sunrise in Yellowstone. Water is essential to a cold-adapted Siberian species such as the bison, and its scarcity in the southern deserts of North America prevented bison from colonizing South America. (Photo © Alan and Sandy Carey)*

MEDICINE MAN AND BUFFALO MANITOU ROCK PAINTING
Page 37, inset: *A buffalo manitou passes medicine to a healer, depicted by the lines running between the spirit animal and the medicine man. The painting is of unknown origin and is believed to date from the precontact era. The original appears on a rock face above a lake at Cow Narrows, Saskatchewan.*

reptiles, amphibians, and invertebrates. Paleo-Indians were so in need of fat to supplement their new diet that they did all they could to extract fat deposits from the large herbivores they were able to kill. They even crushed the bones into small pieces and boiled them to collect all the fat possible. Crushed bones included particles from the feet and lower jaw bones, which modern Inuit from the north slope of Alaska report that they smash only under hardship conditions.

Other vestiges of native life also reveal hunger, such as asymmetries in the growth of the skeletons of hunter-gatherers as compared with agriculturists. In Canada's northern forests the hardship of native life was reflected in poor body growth. Explorer David Thompson, who traveled through western North America in the late 1700s, ascribes differences in physical stature to the hunting economy of Native Canadian tribes. Those suffering most hardships, such as those living close to Hudson Bay, were relatively small of stature, while those living inland and enjoying a better life, such as the bison-hunting plains Indians, were taller and well developed. Significantly, the first Native American tribe to convert totally to the horse culture was the Comanches, a tribe of hunter-gatherers from the Wyoming foothills of the Rockies. Pre-Columbian archaeological finds here suggest a lifestyle of hunger and deprivation. The Commanches were a small-bodied people, a reflection of hardship; moreover, their body size did not grow substantially larger despite later living well off bison.

Native North Americans soon began to manage game in parts of the continent to assure a supply of food during times of shortages. In places, they fed game to attract and hold animals; in the southeastern part of the continent, they deliberately set fire to vegetation to create forage for deer and other game. In coastal Alaska, where brown bears were hunted severely, natives set aside certain salmon streams for bear use; this controlled bear movement and made encounters more predictable both for hunting and for a community's safety. Some eastern tribes even created family-owned plots to manage game.

Living on Bison

Native hunters who lived off buffalo were faced with capricious movement of bison, which made planning difficult. On the bison range, blue camas bulbs became an important human staple, augmented by various roots and berries. Primitive agriculture practiced by some plains tribes such as the Mandan was an attempt to counteract the unpredictability and unreliability of bison as a food supply.

The Mandan's location on the Missouri River was also perfect for recovering carcasses of drowned bison, which supplied a significant amount of welcome food. As speedy, enduring runners, bison choose smooth, flat surfaces for security, and there are few surfaces smoother and flatter than ice on lakes and rivers. When the ice is still thin in fall, or when it thaws in spring, bison may drown en masse. When Europeans arrived, drowned bison were a common sight in spring along prairie rivers and were a dependable food source for carnivores and natives alike. In spring 1801, Canadian fur trader Alexander Henry the Younger recorded masses of drowned bison drifting with broken ice during the break-up of the Red River, their deposition in large numbers along the

Hunters dressed as wolves
Indians camouflaged beneath wolf pelts and armed with bows and arrows crawl toward a herd of buffalo. As George Catlin wrote, "buffalo are aware of their own superiority in combined force, and seem to have no dread of the wolf. . . . The Indian profits by these circumstances by placing himself under the skin of a white wolf, with his weapons in hand, in which plight he often creeps over the level prairies (where there is no object to conceal him) to close company with the unsuspecting herd." (Courtesy of the Library of Congress)

riverbank, and the subsequent putrefaction and stench: "The river clear of ice, but drowned buffalo continue to drift by in entire herds. . . . The women cut up some of the fattest for their own use; the flesh appeared to be fresh and good." Grizzly bears gathered along rivers in spring to partake of the feast, making boat travel hazardous at times, and Native North Americans kept a lookout for bloated bison carcasses drifting by. During his travels up the Missouri River in 1833–1834, German explorer Prince Maximilian zu Wied observed the Mandan driving bison onto thin river ice, where the buffalo fell through and were swept under the ice by the current. Other hunters waited at ice-free spots downstream to secure the carcasses, drag them ashore, and let them "ripen" prior to consumption.

Hardship in the lower latitudes in pre-Columbian North America caused depressed populations of bison, elk, and probably black bear; some species, such as moose, were regionally extinct. It is likely that the bison's unpredictable movements, plus their Great Plains habitat, inhospitable to human hunters, saved them from extinction. Given the hunger and hardships revealed at archaeological sites, bison would have been exterminated had they not removed themselves from the reach of human hunters.

During the Holocene era, about 10,000 years ago, human hunters confined bison to the Great Plains, keeping them away from the richer forage of the western foothills and the eastern river systems. Compared with wood bison from lush meadows in the northern forests at this time, bison on the Great Plains suffered from poor nutrition; however, plains bison

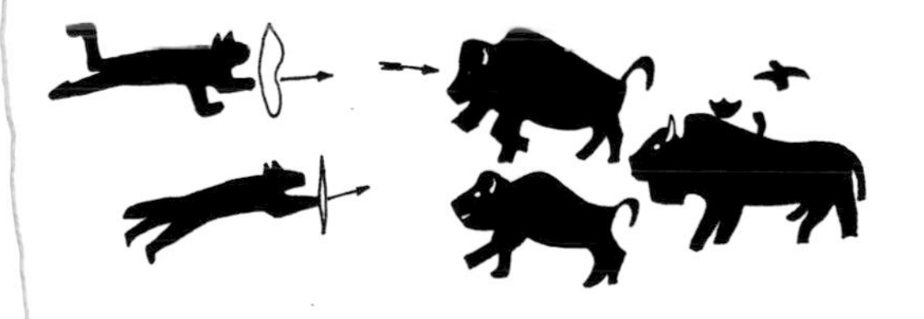

Hidatsa buffalo hunting pictograph
This drawing by Hidatsa Chief Lean Wolf shows hunters hidden beneath wolf pelts approaching a herd of buffalo.

SAULTEAUX OR PLAINS CREE BUFFALO HEAD EFFIGY

This buffalo effigy was made from a carved wooden base wrapped in hand-tanned bison hide; beadwork covering the rawhide details a buffalo's facial features. This amulet is believed to have been used by Saulteaux or Plains Cree hunters in locating buffalo; it may have been worn in the Buffalo Dance and the Thirst Dance. (Artifact #H88.94.153; Ethnology Program, Provincial Museum of Alberta, Edmonton, Canada)

Pte, the buffalo, provided just about everything [the Indians] needed, right down to his tail which made a splendid fly whisk. Fresh meat, tallow, warm robes, leggings, bow strings, bone needles, battle shields and coracles from his tough hide, axes and hoes from his shoulder blades, sledge runners from his ribs, glue from his boiled hooves, red paint from his blood, fuel from his dung, ladles from his horns, hair to stuff pillows, and so on. They even used his long black beard to ornament their cloths. Therefore they addressed him as Uncle, this useful monster, and followed him across the seasons.

—*Evan S. Connell,* Son of the Morning Star

that were venturesome and left the security of the big herds on the plains to go where forage was better—and people were more abundant—were soon killed off. Venturesome bison, those with *dispersal*-type characteristics, are expected to be large in body. Consequently, the bison that had the best chance of survival and reproduction were the smaller, underdeveloped ones—those with *maintenance*-type features. These are the bison that typically stay in big herds and make do with limited forage on the central plains. Thus, it was fear that kept bison in the safety of open spaces and in the security of the herds.

This process of removing larger, more adventurous bison that ventured away from the Great Plains, repeated millennium after millennium, made for small bison with better teeth for cutting and grinding poor forage and for individuals that sought safety in the herd. Frequent migrations to find new pastures after droughts, blizzards, icing, and fires, and competition for grazing areas among members of the herd, meant that individual bison expended vast amounts of energy just to find food—limiting net gains in energy, necessary for growth. Therefore, migratory plains bison could only be small bison, just as migratory caribou are small compared with sedentary caribou.

The human predators bison contended with were not fast, but human hunters were supremely enduring and tenacious in pursuit; they could see far distances, had an excellent memory, and could deceive by approaching in various disguises. Bison could minimize contact with human hunters by way of unpredictable, random movements by large herds in the sea of space that was the Great Plains. Where humans were scare, bison could also escape hunters by quickly hiding and unpredictably moving in a sea of trees. In the north, bison survived at a low density on meadows within forests; large, non-migratory, woodland-type bison developed here, which the continuous hunting pressure kept shy, nervous, and dispersed.

Hunting Buffalo

Before the arrival of the horse in the 1600s, native hunters used a variety of means to kill bison. Before the days of the horse, buffalo hunting was much more difficult.

One early method of bison hunting was based on a shrewd tactic of imitating wolves because buffalo lived in the safety of herds and tended to tolerate wolves. By using wolf skins for disguises, native hunters could approach bison to within shooting range of their bows. Canadian Blood Indian Mike Oka recounted: "The Bloods hunted on foot with bow and arrows before they had horses. They threw wolf skins over their shoulders, then crawled on hands and knees across the ground towards the buffalo. The buffalo often mistook them for coyotes. When they were close enough they would select their animal and shoot it with bow and arrow." Canadian sheriff Alexander Ross told in *The Remarkable History of the Hudson's Bay Company* from 1900 of Canadian Métis using the wolf tactic in winter: "In deep snow, where horses cannot conveniently be used, dogs are very serviceable animals to the [Métis] hunters in these parts. The half-breed, dressed in his wolf costume, tackles two or three sturdy curs into a flat sled, throws himself on it at full length, and gets among the buffalo unperceived. Here the bow and arrow play their part to prevent noise. And here the skillful hunter kills as many as he pleases, and returns to camp without disturbing the band."

Other hunting methods involved ambushing whole herds of bison. Blood Mike Oka remembered such ambushes: "[The Blood formed] into two long rows of men lying flat on their stomachs under the cover of night. The two rows of men stretched for miles sometimes, and led towards a cut bank or steep coulee. About sunrise some braves would stampede the buffalo between the two rows of men. In their mad charge the buffalo pushed their leaders over the bank, while many others were killed with bow and arrows." During his travels in Illinois in 1683, Father Louis Hennepin witnessed a similar hunt, as told in his chronicle *A New Discovery of a Vast Country in America* published in 1903: "When the Savages discover a great Number of those beasts together, they likewise assembled their whole Tribe to encompass the Bulls, and then set on fire the dry Herbs about them, except in some places which they leave free; and therein lay themselves in Ambuscade. The Bulls seeing the Flame round about them, run away through those Passages where they see no

"Chasse Générale au Boeuf mais a pièd," 1700s
This engraving depicts a buffalo hunt by Natchez Indians on foot in the Louisiana Territory, showing the strategy of encircling a small herd before striking with bows and arrows. This image was drawn by Antoine S. Le Page Du Pratz and appeared in his three-volume Histoire de la Louisiane, *printed in Paris in 1758.*

▲▲▲ Native North American Legends ▲▲▲

Origins of the Buffalo Jump

Joseph Medicine Crow, a Montana Crow, told this story crediting Old Man Coyote, the creator of the world and teacher of the Crow, with giving them the idea of running buffalo over cliffs. Medicine Crow's story was reprinted in *Montana Archaeological Society Memoir* No. 1 (May 1962).

OLD MAN COYOTE was hungry one day and so were the rest of the people, and he decided to go look for some meat. Soon he found a herd of buffalo upon a bench. He decided to trick them, over a nearby cliff hidden by a thick cloud or fog. In his usual bragging style, he challenged the head buffalo to a race. Well, as the story goes, immediately his challenge was accepted and the race was on. Naturally Old Man Coyote selected the course, was ahead, and when they approached the cliff, he disappeared quickly. The buffalo herd went over the cliff. Old Man Coyote jumped around to the lower end and returned with his clothing all messed up, if he was wearing clothing; maybe he changed himself into a buffalo. Anyway, he made his nose bleed and pretended like he was hurt. The inference of this little legend was that buffalo were driven over cliffs a long, long time ago by the Crow Indians.

fire; and there fall into the Hands of the Savages who by these Means will kill sometimes above sixscore in a day."

Another effective hunting method was to drive small bison herds into a corral, where they were quickly slaughtered. Canadian Plains Cree Edward Ahenakew told of building the pounds: "They cut trees to make a circular pound about seventy yards across. The trees were big, and they braced them on the outside for extra strength. They set heavy gate-posts, with a cross-bar above, and they hung an old buffalo skull there, that rattled in the wind. The gate was fourteen feet wide, and out from it they laid two long lines of tufted willows that spread farther and farther apart, to channel the buffalo into the pound. In the centre they set a great lobbed tree. . . . Far on the plain, a herd of buffalo was sighted, and two young men rode out to watch. They were to blow their whistles as soon as the buffalo started to move in the early morning. Other men went out to hide behind drifts of snow, and when the sun was high we heard yells that the buffalo were coming. The buffalo were spread out in a long line, and the noise of their coming was like thunder. Whenever they swung too far one way or the other, the men who were hidden on that side would jump up and yell, '*O-oh-whi!*' and fire their guns. The buffalo came on between the lines of willow and through the gate, and they circled round and round the lobbed tree at the centre until the pound was filled. Then the hunters closed in, and stopped the gateway with poles and buffalo robes."

No buffalo-hunting method was more spectacular, however, than skillfully maneuvering bison herds over cliffs. While bison occasionally and accidentally stampeded over cliffs, the systematic herding of bison over "jumps" was a difficult feat to engineer. It required meticulous planning and organization by the tribe as a whole and included extensive ritual and spiritual preparation.

To insure success, it was necessary to start a bison herd down a runway toward a hidden drop off to keep the unsuspecting bison on a steady run in a compact herd, to prevent any attempt by the herd to deviate from that run, to run the whole herd over the cliff to the last animal, and to kill any bison that might have survived the plunge so that no bison escaped. Young men skillful in imitating bison or wolves started the herd down the runway. Flanking the runway were stone cairns topped by branches, behind which hunters hid. At the appropriate time, these hunters rose to spook the bison in the desired direction. Each cairn thus became a source of fright

"Buffalo Drive"
Hunters on foot and horseback drive buffalo over a jump in this dramatic oil painting of 1947 by William Robinson Leigh. This nostalgic vision is a bit of a historic anomaly: After horses arrived in North America, native hunters created new hunting strategies and no longer had to rely on the laborious and difficult tactics of driving buffalo over cliffs. (Courtesy of the Buffalo Bill Historical Center, Cody, WY)

to the bison, ensuring that they were unlikely to deviate from the chosen path. The land had to rise slightly just before the cliff, obscuring any view of the drop. The bison, running flat out, had no warning about the change in the lay of the land and plunged to their deaths. Those that survived were quickly dispatched with clubs and lances by hunters waiting at the base of the cliff.

Europeans who observed natives hunting buffalo often castigated them for killing bison in a herd to the last animal, even though not all of the bison were subsequently utilized. Why kill if you do not need to? Why waste? Yet native people had sound reasons to act as they did. Large mammals are excellent learners and are ruthlessly logical in their responses. A bison who discovers that it can evade those that herd it, or who discovers that it can easily crash through flimsy corrals, will in the future evade hunters and crash through corrals. Thus it is imperative that no bison escape a drive, a surround, or a pound. If it does, the whole hunting enterprise becomes inefficient, not enough meat is procured, and the hunting group suffers. As Canadian Northwest Company fur trader Alexander Henry the Younger

Buffalo herd on the move
Bison are capable runners, and only a good horse had the speed and stamina to outrun buffalo. Such horses were cherished and highly valued among the plains Indians. (Photo © Layne Kennedy)

I go to kill the buffalo
The Great Spirit sent the buffalo
On hills, in plains and woods
So give me my bow, give me my bow
I go to kill the buffalo
—*Sioux song*

recounted in his *Journals* of 1806, "[The Mandans] are anxious to prevent the buffalo from being driven away. For this purpose it is customary for them all in a body to surround one herd only, which sometimes consists of several hundreds. Not one of the herd do they allow to escape; large and small, fat and lean, all must fall, to prevent alarming other herds." Indeed, European observers reported that some bison did escape from herding and pounds, and corrals began to lose their effectiveness as herded bison avoided them. Some historians believe that Native North Americans also killed in excess to reduce the number of bison available to other tribes or white hunters they competed against.

Native hunters' concern that buffalo not learn the "wrong" response is evident again and again in comments of early observers. Explorer John Bradbury came across this among the Mandans, as recounted in his journals of 1809–1811: "Went early to the bluffs to the south-westward of town, on one of which I observed fourteen buffalo skulls placed in a row. The cavities of the eyes and the nostrils were filled with a species of *artemisia* common on the prairies, which appears to be a nondescript. On my return, I told our interpreter to inquire into the reason of this,

Pishkun, The Buffalo Jump

During the travels of Captains Meriwether Lewis and William Clark to find a northwest passage to the Pacific Ocean, Lewis wrote about the buffalo jump and how the Native Americans herded the bison to the precipice. He spotted this jump along the Musselshell River in what would become Montana and wrote of it in *The Journals of Lewis and Clark* on May 29, 1805.

Today we passed on the Stard. side the remains of a vast many mangled carcasses of Buffalow which had been driven over a precipice of 120 feet by the Indians and perished; the water appeared to have washed away a part of this immense pile of slaughter and still their remained the fragments of at least a hundred carcases. They created a most horrid stench. In this manner the Indians of the Missouri [River] distroy vast herds of buffaloe at a stroke; for this purpose one of the most active and fleet young men is selected and disguised in a robe of buffaloe skin, having also the skin of the buffaloe's head with the ears and horns fastened on his head in form of a cap, thus caparisoned he places himself at a convenient distance between a herd of buffaloe and a precipice proper for the purpose, which happens in many places on this river for miles together; the other Indians now surround the herd on the back and flanks and at a signal agreed on all show themselves at the same time moving forward toward the buffaloe: the disguised Indian or decoy has taken care to place himself sufficiently nigh the buffaloe to be noticed by them when they take to flight and running before them they follow him in full speede to the precipice, the cattle behind driving those in front over and seeing them go do not look or hesitate about following until the whole are precipitated down the precepice forming one mass of dead and mangled carcasses; the decoy in the mean time has taken care to secure himself in some cranney or crivice of the clift which he had previously prepared for that purpose. The part of the decoy I am informed is extreamly dangerous, if they are not very fleet runers the buffaloe tread them under foot and crush them to death, and sometimes drive them over the precipice also, where they perish in common with the buffaloe.

Head-Smashed-In buffalo jump
The long outcropping of sandstone cliffs at Head-Smashed-In on the edge of Alberta's Porcupine Hills provided an ideal "jump" for buffalo hunters. Archaeologists believe bison were first driven to their death over the cliffs as long ago as 5,500 years ago. (Photo © Winston Fraser)

Buffalo jump
A fanciful drawing of Indians on horseback running a gigantic herd of bison over a large buffalo jump. (Courtesy of the National Archives of Canada)

The Buffalo Dance

During his travels across North America, George Catlin lived for a time with the Mandans on the Upper Missouri in 1830s and witnessed their dance to make the buffalo come. He described it in detail in his *Letters and Notes on the Manners, Customs, and Condition of the North American Indians*, published in 1842.

THEY DANCE TO induce the buffalo herds to change the directions of their wanderings, to bend their course toward the Mandan village, to graze about on the beautiful hills and bluffs in its vicinity, where the Mandan can shoot them down and cook them as they want for food.

By riding out a mile or two from the village, for most of the year, the young warriors and hunters can kill meat in abundance. But when the young men range the country as far as they are willing to risk their lives, on account of their enemies, without finding meat, the chiefs and doctors sit in solemn council and consult on the measures to be taken, until they decide upon the old and only expedient which "never has failed."

The chief issues his orders to his runners or criers, who proclaim it through the village, and in a few minutes the dance begins. The place where this strange operation is carried on is in the public area in the center of the village, and in front of the great medicine or mystery lodge. About ten or fifteen Mandans at a time join in the dance, each one with the skin of the buffalo's head (or mask), with the horns on, placed over his head, and in his hands his favorite bow or lance, with which he is used to slay the buffalo.

The dance always has the desired effect. It never fails. Nor can it, for it cannot be stopped, going incessantly day and night until "buffalo come." Drums beat and rattles shake, songs and yells are shouted, and lookers-on stand ready with masks on their heads and weapons in hand

PLAINS CREE BUFFALO DANCE HEADDRESS
Above: *This buffalo headdress was worn by a Plains Cree man who died in 1933 at the age of one hundred. While wearing this headdress during a Buffalo Dance, he would assume qualities of the buffalo. The Plains Cree are believed to have acquired the Buffalo Dance tradition from the Dakota at a time when the Cree and Dakota were camped together on the South Saskatchewan River in the 1800s. Cartridge shells served as ornamentation to the bonnet. (Artifact #H72.176.1b; Ethnology Program, Provincial Museum of Alberta, Edmonton, Canada)*

"MAKING THE BUFFALO COME"
Right: *George Catlin's early 1800s sketch of the Mandan buffalo dance.*

to take the place of each dancer as he becomes fatigued, and jumps out of the ring.

During this time of general excitement, spies or "lookers" are kept on the hills in the neighborhood of the village. When they sight buffaloes, they give the signal by "throwing their robes," which is instantly seen in the village and understood by the whole tribe. At this joyful intelligence there is a shout of thanks to the Great Spirit, and more especially to the mystery-man, and the dancers, who have been the immediate cause of their success!

These dances sometimes continue two or three weeks without stopping an instant, until the joyful moment when buffaloes made their appearance. So they *never fail*; and they believe the dance has been the means of bringing the buffalo.

The mask worn by these dancers is put over the head, and generally has a strip of the skin hanging to it, of the whole length of the animal, with the tail attached to it. The skin passes down over the back of the dancer, dragging on the ground. When one dancer becomes fatigued, he bends forward, sinking his body towards the ground. Another draws a bow upon him and hits him with a blunt arrow. The exhausted dancer falls like a buffalo, is seized by the bystanders, and dragged out of the ring by the heels. The bystanders brandish their knives about him, and go through the motions of skinning and cutting him up. Then they let him off, and his place is at once supplied by another, who dances into the ring with his mask on. By this taking of places the scene is easily kept up night and day until "the buffalo come."

HUNTING BISON IN SNOW
George Catlin's early 1800s sketch depicts Mandan Indians running across the top of the snow on snowshoes to hunt buffalo in the winter. The bison are mired in the snow, making them easy targets.

and learned that it was an honour conferred by the Indians on the buffaloes which they had killed, in order to appease their spirits, and prevent them from apprising the living buffaloes of the danger they run in approaching the neighbourhood." In addition, if bison were in the vicinity of a settlement, great care was taken not to disturb them. If hunting did take place, it was conducted so that the bison did not witness the kill. Special "soldiers" were appointed by some tribes to police against hunting by individuals, which might frighten away the buffalo and reduce availability to the tribe. Some of the early missionaries remarked on the tameness of the bison; wild animals grow tame only if unmolested.

European observers also commented on the wastefulness of the native hunters' butchering practices. Excluding the killing for trade, the main reason Native North Americans killed bison was to obtain food. Eating only lean meat is dangerous, yet Indians were almost entirely dependent on meat from game animals, with plant food playing a variable role, and in the case of plains Indians subsisting on buffalo, an insignificant one. The butch-

At last the day came when my father allowed me to go on a buffalo hunt with him. And what a proud boy I was! Ever since I could remember my father had been teaching me the things that I should know and preparing me to be a good hunter. I had learned to make bows and to string them; and to make arrows and tip them with feathers. I knew how to ride my pony no matter how fast he would go, and I felt that I was brave and did not fear danger. All these things I had learned for just this day when father would allow me to go with him on a buffalo hunt. It was the event for which every Sioux boy eagerly waited.

—Luther Standing Bear,
My Indian Boyhood*, 1931*

Gros Ventre buffalo-horn headdress
Made in the 1880s of buffalo hide and surmounted by bison horns, this Gros Ventre headdress was adorned with eagle feathers, brass bells, and human hair. (Courtesy of the Buffalo Bill Historical Center, Cody, WY; Gift of Mr. and Mrs. Larry Larom)

ering practices reflect this need for fat.

Not all buffalo are equally fat. Females in late spring and during lactation in summer may be low in fat, as are young animals accompanying adults in winter and bulls for weeks following the strains of the mating season. Consequently, in any assembly of bison killed in a pound or at a jump site, there were bison with little body fat. These animals were not worth butchering as they were not worth eating—their lean, depleted muscle meat was actually dangerous to eat. Nor was there any fat to be extracted from their abdominal cavity or long bones. Often times only the tongue was taken because tongues retain some fat, as Hudson's Bay Company explorer Samuel Hearne noted during his travels across Canada in 1769 to 1772: "The tongue is also very delicate; and what is most extraordinary, when the beasts are in the poorest state, which happens regularly at certain seasons, their tongues are then very fat and fine; some say, fatter than when they are in the best order." Some bison were only partially butchered, so that the fat portions were extracted while parts with little fat were left. As in so many other instances, European reactions of the time were based on an incomplete understanding of the forces at work.

Bison Biology

A drawback to herd life is competition for forage. Where many feed, little food remains. This makes some herd members take chances, depending on their vulnerability to predation. The better a bison is at evading predators, the more chances it can take with security in favor of food. Large, healthy bulls are least vulnerable, while calves are most vulnerable. Consequently, cows and calves compromise food

in favor of security, while bulls compromise security in favor of food. The bulls have little choice because growing large in body is a prerequisite for social, and thus reproductive, success. As growing large is mainly a matter of getting all the food required for growth, bulls stay in small groups, forage far apart, chose ground difficult to run on—just so long as there is richer forage to be had. Cows, by contrast, seek hard, dry, unobstructed ground in order to run efficiently, group into large herds, and stay close together.

Competition for forage pulls male and female bison into different habitats and therefore different body sizes; however, it also draws them together in external appearance. In winter and deep snow, bison must clear snow to feed, which entails much labor. One way to minimize labor is to pirate the work of others by displacing them from craters and feeding on the forage there. Young bulls have the most to gain from this as they have little reproductive interest in the females. Large breeding bulls have the least to gain from pirating female labor, provided they have inseminated the cows; to compete for food with the mothers of their offspring would run counter to their reproductive interests. To ward off young bulls, cow bison must be large and aggressive enough to discourage them; to do this, it helps to look like a bull. In many social ungulates, females resemble males of an age at which the males separate from the female herds to go off with other males. With bison bulls, this separation happens at three to four years of age.

For bison bulls of all ages, life in a female herd appears to be safe. Keeping within cow groups is likely the safest option for young bulls where herds are small, population density is low, and predators common. In some species of New World deer and pronghorns, males after rutting shed antlers, horns, and ornamental hair outgrowths, and join female herds. Being slower than females and exhausted from rutting and wounds, large males are susceptible to predation; however, by looking like females when surrounded by females, they may escape detection by predators. Indeed, after the rut, adult bison bulls shed much of their display hair and look more like females.

Bison calves, born to herd life, need to be quick, enduring runners soon after birth to keep up with adults when escaping wolves. Consequently, selection favors single births and large calves that quickly run after birth. At birth, bison weigh 30 to 70 pounds (13.5–31.5 kg), about twice as much as a moose calf, although the mothers of both are nearly the same size. The bison cow's milk is rich in solids, which allows for rapid growth of the calf to survivable size. Although captive bison tend to bear young every year, in wild herds births may be less frequent.

American bison are adapted to feed on the short, dense grasses of the short-grass prairie. They have broad incisors that allow them a wide bite on short grass, and large molars and premolars because of the great wear and tear on teeth by dusty, coarse grasses in a largely arid landscape. Bison are able to utilize tough-fibered, low-protein grasses because a large fraction of their urea, the end-product of protein digestion, is circulated back into the rumen, or primary stomach, via the saliva rather than excreted within the urine. This recycling gives the bacteria in the bison's digestive system more nitrogen to incorporate into their own bodies. Consequently,

ANISHINABE BUFFALO PETROGLYPH
An Anishinabe (Ojibway or Chippewa) effigy of a bison carved into the rock wall of "The Pictured Cave," also known as Brown's Cavern, near La Crosse, Wisconsin.

For animals which perform no labor, they have an egregious appetite, eating as if they were Nature's lawn-gardeners, and were under contract with her to keep the grass shaved.
—*W.E. Webb,* Buffalo Land, *1872*

The Buffalo Corral

In the days before the horse made its dramatic entry into the plains Indians' life, hunting buffalo was done with stealth or organization. As with buffalo jumps, building a corral or pound to trap buffalo required extensive labor, planning, and luck. Northwest Company fur trader Alexander Henry the Younger described in detail in his *Journals* how the Assiniboine of the Ontario and Saskatchewan plains hunted buffalo in 1808 with a corral:

IT IS SUPPOSED that these people are the most expert and dexterous nation of the plains in constructing pounds, and in driving buffalo into them. The pounds are of different dimensions, according to the number of tents in one camp. The common size is from 60 to 100 paces or yards in circumference, and about five feet in height. Trees are cut down, laid upon one another, and interwoven with branches and green twigs; small openings are left to admit the dogs to feed upon the carcasses of the bulls, which are generally left as useless. This inclosure is commonly made between two hummocks, on the declivity or at the foot of rising ground. The entrance is about ten paces wide, and always fronts the plains. On each side of this entrance commences a thick range of fascines, the two ranges spreading asunder as they extend, to the distance of 100 yards, beyond which openings are left at intervals; but the fascines soon become more thinly planted, and continue to spread apart to the right and left, until each range has been extended about 300 yards from the pound. The labor is then diminished by only placing at intervals three or four cross-sticks, in imitation of a dog or other animal [sometimes called "dead men"]; these extend on the plain for about two miles, and double rows of them are planted in several other directions to a still greater distance. Young men are usually sent out to collect and bring in the buffalo—a tedious task which requires great patience, for the herd must be started by slow degrees. This is done by setting fire to dung or grass. Three young men will bring a herd of several hundred from a great distance. When the wind is aft it is most favorable, as they can then direct the buffalo with great ease. Having come in sight of the ranges, they generally drive the herd faster, until it begins to enter the ranges, where a swift-footed person has been stationed with a buffalo robe over his head, to imitate that animal; but sometimes a horse performs this business. When he sees buffaloes approaching, he moves slowly toward the pound until they appear to follow him; then he sets off at full speed, imitating a buffalo as well as he can, with the herd after him. The young men in the rear now discover themselves, and drive the herd on with all possible speed. There is always a sentinel on some elevated spot to notify the camp when the buffalo appear; and this intelligence is no sooner given than every man, woman, and child runs to the ranges that lead to the pound, to prevent the buffalo from taking a wrong direction. There they lie down between the fascines and cross-sticks, and if the buffalo attempt to break through, the people wave their robes, which causes the herd to keep on, or turn to the opposite side, where other persons do the same. When the buffalo have been thus directed to the entrance of the pound, the Indian who leads them rushes into it and out at the other side, either by jumping over the inclosure or creeping through an opening left for that purpose. The buffalo tumble pell-mell at his heels, almost exhausted, but keep moving around the inclosure from E. to W., and never in a direction against the sun. What appeared extraordinary to me, on those occasions, was that, when word was given to the camp of the near approach of the buffalo, the dogs would skulk away from the pound, and not approach until the herd entered. Many buffaloes break their legs, and some their necks, in jumping into the pound, as the descent is generally six to eight feet, and stumps are left standing there. The buffalo being caught, the men assemble at the inclosure, armed with bows and arrows; every arrow has a particular mark of the owner, and they fly until the whole herd is killed. Then the men enter the pound, and each claims his own; but commonly there is what they term the master of the pound, who divides the animals and gives each tent an equal share, reserving nothing for himself. But in the end he is always the best provided for; everyone is obliged to send him a certain portion, as it is in his tent that the numerous ceremonies relating to the pound are observed. There the young men are always welcome to feast and smoke, and no women are allowed to enter, as that tent is set apart for the affairs of the pound. Horses are sometimes used to collect and bring in buffalo, but this method is less effectual than the other; besides, it frightens the herds and soon causes them to withdraw to a great distance. When horses are used, the buffalo are absolutely driven into the pound; but when the other method is pursued, they are in a manner enticed to their destruction.

In 1912, Canadian Cree Joseph F. Dion began writing down the life of his ancestors, practices that were passed down to him by word of mouth. He wrote of the pound style of hunting buffalo and the key role of the poundmaker in his memoir, *My Tribe the Crees*:

ALL THE TIME the work of building was going on the poundmaker was in a state of prayer. He sang and beat on a drum for some time every night, beseeching the Father of All to assist him in enticing the buffalo to enter his pound willingly. When all was ready, he started out alone to round up a herd sufficiently large to fill the corral. The man carried nothing but his buffalo robe. He depended mostly on his own speed and staying power. It is strange but true that a poundmaker could always drive the herd he wanted safely into the enclosure without much assistance. Care was always taken not to stampede the animals until they had entered the upper part of the V-shaped fence. As the buffaloes tumbled into the main pound, much rejoicing was manifested for then a plentiful supply of food and hides was ensured for all. There were times when the kill was so large that it was impossible for the people to handle everything, hence much good meat was left behind when the camp moved on.

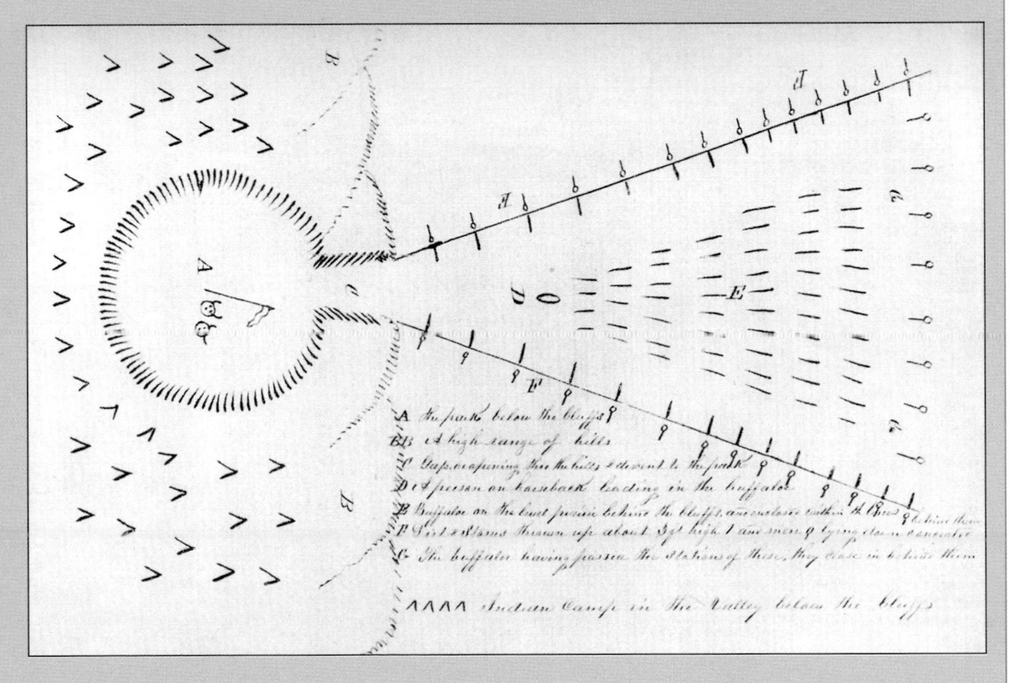

Assiniboin buffalo surround
Details for the layout of an Assiniboin Sioux buffalo surround, as drawn by Edwin T. Denig about 1854. Runners lured and directed the herd into the funnel leading to the corral; other hunters hid behind the funnel walls, frightening the bison along their way into the pound.

Then when we had come near to where the bison were, the hunters circled around them, and the cry went up, as in a battle, "Hoka hey!" which meant to charge. Then there was a great dust and everybody shouted and all the hunters went in to kill—every man for himself. They were all nearly naked, with their quivers full of arrows hanging on their left sides, and they would ride right up to a bison and shoot him behind the left shoulder. Some of the arrows would go in up to the feathers and sometimes those that struck no bones went straight through. Everybody was very happy.

. . . I was not old enough to hunt. So we little boys scouted around and watched the hunters; and when we would see a bunch of bison coming, we would yell "Yuhoo" like the others, but nobody noticed us. When the butchering was all over, they hung the meat across the horses' backs and fastened it with strips of fresh bison hide. On the way back to the village all the hunting horses were loaded, and we little boys who could not wait for the feast helped ourselves to all the raw liver we wanted. . . . The women were busy cutting the meat into strips and hanging it on the racks to dry. You could see red meat hanging everywhere. The people feasted all night long and danced and sang. Those were happy times.

—*Oglala Sioux holy man Black Elk telling of his first buffalo hunt,* Black Elk Speaks, *1932*

The buffalo bull is one of the most formidable and frightful-looking animals in the world when excited to resistance; his long shaggy mane hangs in great profusion over his neck and shoulders, and often extends quite down to the ground. The cow is less in stature and less ferocious, though not much less wild and frightful in her appearance.

—*George Catlin, living with the Mandans on the Upper Missouri in 1830s,* Letters and Notes on the Manners, Customs, and Condition of the North American Indians, *1842*

BUFFALO WALLOW

A bison bull dusts itself in a wallow in the Lamar Valley of Yellowstone National Park. During spring and summer, shortly after shedding, the North American bison bull grows a display coat—or robe—on the front of the body while the rear of the body remains thinly haired and poorly insulated. The robe is light on top, with dark colors at the lower parts and underside of the body. The front of the bison is black, a trait shared by virtually all large herbivores that confront predators. (Photo © Erwin and Peggy Bauer)

a bison can maintain a larger amount of bacteria and protozoa in its rumen and can better ferment coarse-fibered vegetation. The bacteria and protozoa are digested in the true stomach and their protein, carbohydrates, fats, and vitamins become incorporated into the bison's body. The digestive system of a bison must also be able to adjust to the ever-changing forage conditions of the seasons.

Despite their sparse forage, the Great Plains have advantages for bison searching for food. Grasses grown in the alkaline soil of the prairies contain metabolic salts such as sodium, magnesium, calcium, and sulfur, which is one reason why bison from the Great Plains did not seek out mineral licks, whereas bison that penetrated into the eastern forests did. So many bison and elk visited such places as the Big Bone Lick in Kentucky in the mid-1700s that they caused considerable land erosion. Also, the low levels of snow fall, infrequent snowstorms, and warm Chinook winds on the plains ensure the sparse vegetation is frequently exposed. This is important as bison do not paw away snow as horses do; rather they sweep away snow with their hairy heads, which works well only when the snow is fine and soft. Bison experience difficulty foraging in the spring when the top layer of snow, melted by the sun during the day, freezes rock hard at night. This "sun crust" can be virtually impenetrable.

Buffalo Wallows

The Great Plains also allow bison bulls plenty of room for indulging in a passion of theirs—wallowing. Bulls love to wallow in summer, be it in dry, dusty soil or in mud, and wallowing vigorously before rivals and females is a method of "display." Cows, on the other hand, wallow relatively little.

In the 1700s and 1800s, wallowing bison in large rutting herds could obscure the herd in a permanent cloud of dust. George Catlin, the keen-eyed artist, gave an excellent description of wallowing: A bison bull made a wallow in water-logged, soft earth by going down upon one knee and gouging a hole with its horn. It lowered itself into the hole and rested flat on its side. The bull then rubbed its hump violently in the soil, opened up the ground by rotating in the wallow, and rolled around lifting its legs upward with great kicks. The bull sank deeper into mud until soon the bull was totally covered with mud "which changes his color, and drips in streams from every part of him as he rises upon his feet, a hideous monster of mud and ugliness."

Whatever protection from biting flies the mud may give the bull's near-naked rear-half, wallowing was primarily a social ritual among bulls. If one bull started to wallow, the most dominant bull was sure to come and displace him. A dominant bull leaving his wallow was followed by another bull, and another, until the whole bull herd had used the same wallow. The wallow was enlarged and deepened as each bull carried away mud in its coat, and wallows became prominent features of the landscape that outlived the extirpation of bison by decades.

The Rutting and Mating Season

The elaborate wallowing rituals and the search to find food to maintain health and adequate growth are but the prelude to the challenges of reproduction. While the reproductive efforts of cows are spaced over the year, from fertilization to pregnancy,

BATTLING BULLS
Bison bulls fight with each other readily during the mating season in summer—and their fights are fierce and intense. The high rate of wounds during these mating battles selected for a thick, tough skin, which on bulls was much thicker and heavier than on cows. Buffalo leather became highly prized for belts to drive factory machinery, and thus played a role in the early industrialization of North America. (Photo © Alan and Sandy Carey)

BULL FLEHMEN
A bison bull tests a cow's urine to determine if the female is in estrus. For this duty, bulls have a specialized feature in the palate called the Jacobson's organ, which is common in almost all ruminants and vestigial in humans. When a bull peels back his upper lips after licking a cow's urine, he activates this olfactory organ. (Photo © Erwin and Peggy Bauer)

RUTTING DUEL
Both photos: *Bison bulls smash into each other head-on in competition for mating females during the rut. The bellowing of bulls was a constant din calling over the plains during the rut, and the dust clouds raised by bison bulls pawing the dry summer soil before battle, wallowing, or hurling up dust during charges hung like a yellow fog over the prairie in summer, according to some early observers. (Photos © Michael H. Francis)*

birth, lactation, and some post-lactation care of the young, the reproductive efforts of bulls are concentrated into the short mating season. The rest of the year the bulls are preparing for the rut.

Sexual competition for cows is severe, and the sins of the past come to haunt bulls at this time. A bull too slow to leave the security of the maternal herd for more dangerous, but better pastures grows too little in muscle and bone and finds itself outclassed by bolder, bigger bulls. A runty bull must seek to leave its genetic mark as an opportunistic breeder, one who checks the periphery of populations for females entering heat. With luck, it may be the only bull around.

Combat in the rutting season is ferocious. Bulls collide full bore and head-on, holding their heads low over the ground. It is as if the bison is trying to hook upward, but at the same time holding his head low so as to prevent the opponent from hooking under him. The top of the skull is covered by a thick plate of skin and a thick hair mop. The force of the clash is probably caught against the tension of the neck and hump.

Although bulls are protected by an armor of skin, they can still injure each other severely in fights. And as most wounds remain invisible under the cover of hair, it is easy to underestimate the extent of combat damage. Studies on deer indicate that active males sustain on average thirty to fifty wounds per rutting season, with a few suffering over 150 wounds per season. A bison bull's strategy in gaining access to females must be a continuous trade-off: Quick, vigorous engagements lead to much fighting and wounding, to rapid loss of competitive ability, to a long, costly recovery from injuries and stunting of body growth, and to increased attention by predators. Too little engagement is safe but yields little breeding. A bull too large in body burns itself out in a rutting season or two and meets with less success than does a smaller one who is less successful each year, but chalks up many years of breeding.

When the herds were large, at mating time—from late July into early September—the prairies were covered by dust clouds as bulls pawed and rolled, flinging up dry prairie soil, or rushed back and forth in combat, butting heads vigorously. Bison congregated into herds that went on for miles upon miles and emptied the prairie elsewhere of all bison. Bulls closely guarded individual cows until these were bred. This led to continuous flows and wheeling of masses of bison in the breeding herd. Bulls probably followed females closely and, if challenged by a rival, fought quickly and rushed back after their fe-

Mating season
A bison bull mounts a cow in Yellowstone National Park. Being a large mammal whose young had to run from predators virtually from birth, bison had to bear large, well-developed calves. That took a long gestation period of 285 days, as well as concentrating all of the mother's available resources into a single calf at birth. For the calf to be born in early summer as grazing food became available, mating had to take place in the late summer of the preceding year. (Photo © Erwin and Peggy Bauer)

Red buffalo calves
During the first six months of life, buffalo calves have a bright red coat. These two calves play together in Yellowstone National Park. (Photo © Michael H. Francis)

male—much as is found in dense breeding herds of barren-ground caribou.

In the more dispersed bison herds that now remain, approaching competitors are met by the guarding bull with a slow, swaggering gait that exposes the bull's broadside to maximum viewing. This is psychological warfare, an attempt to intimidate the rival with a show of size. Rolling in and horning the wallow displays strength and vigor. All vertebrates, humans included, have a system of complex dominance displays. To reduce the incidence of costly combat, bison use a lot of bluffing to size up opponents and test the determination of competitors. The bulls also bellow, which in large breeding congregations sounds like distant thunder.

Physical appearance is important to the rutting bull. Well-developed secondary sexual organs, which are based on rare amino acids such as those found in hair and can be grown only when the body's maintenance and growth requirements are met, speak of a healthy, strong, capable male. The long hair on a bull's head, neck, and shoulders increases with age as well as with the quality of habitat, reflecting

availability of forage to the bull before the rut. The "shaggier" the bull, the better it has eaten, the better it is at foraging, the more daring it is in taking chances with predators in order to obtain superior forage, and the healthier it is.

The cow-tending bull displays its swaying mass and hair coat not only to rivals. It also places itself before the female, as if showing off. And that's what it likely is. The shaggier the bull, the more likely that it will pass on to its offspring its features as a superior forager and escape-artist. Cows about to mate are attracted to such a bull.

The bull tests the cow's approach to estrus by nuzzling her urine. Then it raises its head and curls its upper lip. This allows a few drops of urine to seep into the Jacobson's organ, a small olfactory pouch in the palate lined with specialized cells that connect directly to the brain. Bulls court cows until they urinate, allowing urine testing. They otherwise stand broadside before the cow, as if blocking her way, showing off. Courtship of the receptive cow involves some licking by the bull and repeated nudging until the cow acquiesces and stands for copulation.

COW AND CALF

A mother buffalo watches over her calf, which still wears its early reddish coat. If a buffalo calf can survive the dangerous first year of life, it has a good chance of living through maturity and growing old. To survive, calves require protection from not only their mother but the entire herd, bulls included. If a calf bawled, bulls swarmed out readily to attack wolves and protect the young. (Photo © Layne Kennedy)

The buffaloes chiefly delight in wide open plains, which in those parts produce very long coarse grass, or rather a kind of small flags and rushes, upon which they feed; but when pursued they always take to the woods. They are of such amazing strength, that when they fly through the woods from a pursuer, they frequently brush down trees as thick as a man's arm; and be the snow ever so deep, such is their strength and agility that they are enabled to plunge through it faster than the swiftest Indian can run in snow-shows. To this I have been an eye-witness many times, and once had the vanity to think that I could have kept pace with them; but though I was at that time celebrated for being particularly fleet of foot in snow-shows, I soon found that I was no match for the buffaloes, notwithstanding they were plunging through such deep snow, that their bellies made a trench in it as large as if many sacks had been hauled through it.

—*Samuel Hearne,* A Journey to The Northern Ocean, *1795*

BISON PICTOGRAPH
This simple buffalo effigy was painted on a rock face near Forest Grove, in central Montana.

In the eighteenth and nineteenth centuries, after the rut the big breeding herds dispersed and bison were found in small groups. Following the peak of milk production and after being bred, the cow almost certainly restores its skeleton, which has been depleted of minerals in order to augment the mineral content of the milk. The muscle tissue is restored, fat is deposited, and vitamins are stored in liver and fat to subsidize meager forage in winter. The embryos have implanted and begin their slow growth in preparation for the birth of calves in late spring, just prior to the plains' bursting into lush, nutritious plant growth. Timing is critical because the demanding task of lactation should occur as close as possible to the time of maximum food supply.

The bulls rest after the rut and recover from injuries. Their effort in the reproductive game may be as great as or greater than that of the females, and they are on "vacation" until the next rutting season. They are thin, having lost most of their stores of fat. Healing wounds and curbing infections drain their body resources even further. They slowly regain condition, grow a winter coat, and begin to add to their body mass. The large bulls form herds of their own away from females. Old bulls, however, which begin to lose interest in rutting, withdraw and may while away the time alone, until they die.

Bison cows withdraw prior to birth, but soon join others, forming nursery groups. Besides adult cows and calves, these groups contain yearlings and a sprinkling of young bulls. A calf spends part of the time with its mother and part of the time with other calves in calf groups. These calf groups may stay together in rest and play, and occasionally follow a single female.

Calves have bright red coats for the first six months of life, after which they grow a dark hair coat, not dissimilar from the adult. In this way, North American bison resemble other highly gregarious ungulates such as caribou and wildebeest: The young has a "uniform" that probably inhibits aggression by unrelated adults in the herd. By contrast, the calf of the European wisent is dark at birth, similar in color to adults. No satisfactory explanation for this difference has been advanced to date.

Buffalo hunters of the nineteenth century became eyewitnesses to various attributes of bison. When calves were still small, disturbing bison resulted in many calves being separated from their mothers. George Catlin records how the calves would try to hide or would follow the mounted hunters to camp. Capturing such a calf and blowing into its nose to transfer the scent of the human conditioned it to trot after its captor. These inadvertent experiments indicate that the calf is highly dependent for its welfare on an attentive mother, as the calf has little capacity to stay with its dam, at least when it is very young. Thus the common practice of the time of killing primarily cows for hides and food not only hurt the future reproductive capacity of the bison population, it also increased calf mortality.

Bison Species and Subspecies

Bison evolved little after the glacial period. When native hunters began using horses to run down bison, there suddenly was severe selection for speed and stamina. This harsh selection began about 1680, when Native Americans in the Southwest became horsemen, and lasted until 1876, when the Battle of the Little Bighorn for all practical purposes sounded the death-knell for the Indian horse culture in the United States. Had it lasted a millennia or more, rather than just two centuries, it might have made the bison as fast as the horse.

There are no subspecies in the species *Bison bison*. Bison were quite similar throughout their range, with the migratory plains bison being somewhat smaller than the sedentary wood bison. In captivity bulls of both forms reach the same body size, and the two forms differ little genetically, if at all. The display hair of bison can vary with the nutritional history of individuals, changing analogously to deer antlers, and this has led to taxonomic confusion. Wood bison have relatively larger humps than plains bison, and female wood bison may be more "bull-like" in external appearance. However, differences between wood and plains bison, if any, are much less than were accepted in the last taxonomic review, by Van Zyll de Jong. Wood and plains bison have a biological reality not as separate subspecies, but as ecotypes whose physical characteristics reflect differences in opportunities and demands placed on them by their respective environments.

The ability of bulls to grow hair coats according to nutritional conditions in summer has caused confusion and trouble in science and management. One taxonomist designated an old bull in a zoo, who had grown a rather inadequate nuptial coat compared with young bulls, as the type specimen of the "southern plains bison." The bull was displaying no more nor less than the old age hair coat of bulls, but it misled the taxonomist into designating bison in Montana as one subspecies and those in the south as another. Northern bison bulls held captive in Elk Island National Park near Edmonton, Alberta, grew

Spanish Conquistadors' Visions of Buffalo

Spanish conquistadors with Hernando Cortez in the early 1500s were the first Europeans to record seeing buffalo in North America. Cortez and the later Spaniards gave dramatic descriptions of these New World monsters for the enlightenment of the people back home.

Cortez and his conquistadors saw a bison in a type of zoo at the palace of Montezuma, the great Aztec ruler, in Anáhuac, now Mexico City. In 1521, Cortez's historian, Antonio de Solis y Rivadeneyra, recorded the Spaniards' vision of this strange and wondrous beast:

In the second Square of the same House were the Wild Beasts, which were either presents to Montezuma, or taken by his Hunters, in strong Cages of Timber, rang'd in good Order, and under Cover: Lions, Tygers, Bears, and all others of the savage Kind which New-Spain produced; among which the greatest Rarity was the Mexican Bull; a wonderful composition of divers Animals. It has crooked Shoulders, with a Bunch on its Back like a Camel; its Flanks dry, its Tail large, and its Neck cover'd with Hair like a Lion. It is cloven footed, its Head armed like that of a Bull, which it resembles in Fierceness, with no less strength and Agility.

In 1542, conquistador Francisco Vásquez de Coronado sighted buffalo in what is now northern New Mexico while searching for the Seven Cities of Cíbola, the seven pueblos the Spaniards believed to contain vast treasures. Like de Solis's account, Coronado's record of the sightings also compares the marvelous beast to known Old World animals:

The first time we encountered the buffalo, all our horses took flight on seeing them, for they are horrible to the sight. They have a broad and short face; eyes two palms from each other, and projecting in such a manner sidewise that they can see a pursuer. Their beard is like that of goats, and so long it drags the ground when they lower the head. They have on the anterior portion of the body a frizzled hair like sheep's wool; it is very fine upon the croup, and sleek like a lion's mane. Their horns are very short and thick, and can scarcely be seen through the hair. They always change their hair in May, and at this season they really resemble lions.

I reached some plains so vast that I did not find their limit anywhere that I went, although I traveled over them for more than 300 leagues. And I found such a quantity of cows [buffalo] . . . that it is impossible to number them, for while I was journeying through these plains, until I returned to where I first found them, there was not a day that I lost sight of them.

American bison, 1500s
The first known depiction by a European of an American bison, this engraving was printed in Francisco Lopez de Gomara's Historia de las Indias, *published in Europe in 1552–1553.*

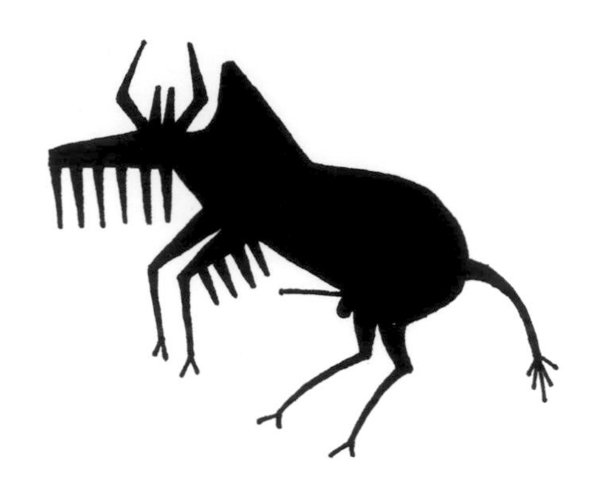

CROW BUFFALO MEDICINE SHIELD EFFIGY
This image of a bull bison was painted on a Crow medicine shield to invoke the animal's power for protection.

These Indians who reside in the large Plains are the most independent and appear to be the happiest and most contented of any People upon the face of the Earth. They subsist on the Flesh of the Buffalo and of the skins they make the greatest part of their cloathing which is both warm and convenient.

—Daniel Harmon, Northwest Company fur trader, journal of 1804

a short hair coat in summer, apparently in response to a scarcity of high-quality feed. These bison were mistakenly identified as of the "wood bison" subspecies. Subsequent research showed that bulls from this herd, transplanted elsewhere and supplied with good nutrition in summer, grew perfectly normal plains bison hair coats.

These examples show that regional differences in large mammals aren't necessarily hereditary, but can be environmental adjustments. This is called *ecotypic adjustment*, and short-haired bison in Elk Island were thus an ecotype, not a subspecies. Ecotypic variation is fleeting, as exemplified by these bison: full summer nutrition transformed "wood bison" into "plains bison." Yet the short-haired coat, a captivity effect, became institutionalized as the type coat for the "wood bison," and bison not showing it were considered atypical by Canadian government scientists. The highly inbred herd at Elk Island became the focus of future bison reintroduction programs as they were considered "wood bison." This was to be a source of considerable controversy when it came to discussions about how to best preserve the bison for the future.

The lack of significant regional subspeciation of bison, despite their wide distribution, is not surprising. Except for the relatively small populations of wood bison on the northern fringes of bison distribution, most bison lived on the great central plains. Here they were confined, artificially, by native hunting pressure. If bison moved about capriciously as evidence strongly suggests, then a constant mixing of hereditary traits north to south and east to west was inevitable. Wood and plains bison may have met along the Peace River as late as 1866, and they probably interbred. There may even have been a small mountain bison, analogous to the small wisent in the Caucasus Mountains, although we have no tangible evidence of its existence. Differences in bison's size, shape, and other external characteristics over the great expanse of their range can be accounted for by normal growth adjustments to differing environmental conditions.

The Heyday of the Herds

By 1480 or earlier, fishermen from Bristol were sailing to the Grand Banks off Newfoundland in the Atlantic Ocean to fish for cod. These fishermen dried and salted their catch on the eastern shores of North America before returning to sell it to Portuguese outlets. They were soon followed to the Grand Banks by ships from Normandy, Brittany, and the Basque provinces. By 1534, a significant traffic had developed, which may have given rise to the subsequent fur trade. These early contacts also brought Eurasian diseases—such as tuberculosis, typhoid, diphtheria, smallpox, whooping cough, influenza, yellow and scarlet fever, and measles—to the native people. These diseases began decimating native people in North America well before various explorers in the sixteenth century made incursions inland.

In the early 1600s, there was massive mortality among the people who had preyed on bison, elk, and bear prior to the arrival of the Europeans. Pandemics probably occurred early in the sixteenth century. Depopulation in the West Indies, Mexico, and Central America was swift before 1600. Old World diseases eliminated many tribes and decimated others, reducing the effects of the native people on the land. The range extension of bison

This scenery already rich pleasing and beautiful was still further hightened by immense herds of Buffaloe, deer Elk and Antelopes which we saw in every direction feeding on the hills and plains. I do not think I exagerate when I estimate the number of Buffaloe which could be compre[hend]ed at one view to amount to 3000.

—*Meriwether Lewis,* The Journals of Lewis and Clark, *September 17, 1804, in the Dakotas*

Buffalo skull medicine
During his travels in the early 1800s, Prince Maximilian zu Wied came across this buffalo-skull monument near the junction of the Yellowstone and Missouri Rivers. Made by Assiniboine hunters, the monument was designed to lure buffalo herds and to ensure a successful hunt.

BUFFALO BULL
George Catlin's early 1800s sketch of a bison bull. Catlin was not only a pioneer painter but also a visionary who foresaw the demise of the bison and the native horse culture on the plains. His sympathy for Indians earned him ridicule and scorn.

All around us, as far as we could see, the plains were black with buffalo. The prairie seemed to be moving.
—*Buffalo hunter Norbert Welsh, as told to Mary Weekes,* The Last Buffalo Hunter, *1931*

east of the Mississippi coincides with the first recorded major smallpox epidemics in the eastern and southern states, as well as with the extinction of native tribes, at least twenty-two of which no longer existed by 1650 and thirty-three of which disappeared by 1690.

With the decline in the Native North American population, bison and elk surged in numbers during the 1600s. Reduced human nest predation allowed passenger pigeons to darken the skies. Salmon left unharvested filled the river and creeks to overflowing. Black bears became abundant. Bison populations underwent a dramatic increase and expanded east and west, often across abandoned Indian land.

The first sightings of bison in the East were recorded in the late 1700s. In the southeastern United States, fields that had been abandoned by Native Americans, which made excellent bison and elk habitat in an otherwise forested country, were common at the time when bison numbers surged there. Spanish conquistador Hernando de Soto traversed parts of the American South in 1539–1542 but recorded no sightings of bison; after 1700, there were reports of bison in many areas covered by de Soto's travels. In the region that later became the state of Mississippi, bison were recorded from 1685 to 1722; in Tennessee, they were abundant from 1764 to 1810; in Kentucky, abundant in 1765, extinct by 1800; in Ohio, present in 1687, abundant by 1750, extinct by 1805; Indiana, present 1718 or earlier, extinct in 1830; in Illinois, abundant in the early 1700s; in Georgia, abundant around 1733, gone by 1770; in the Carolinas, a few were recorded in 1709, abundant by the beginning of the eighteenth century, extinct by 1775; in Virginia, present in 1720, extinct in 1772; in Maryland, recorded from 1632 to 1680.

When bison were numerous in Kentucky and Tennessee around 1750, they gathered near mineral licks. Here, observers noted, they destroyed topsoil to such an extent that old trees showed three to four feet (90–120 cm) of roots, while the underbrush was completely destroyed. This meant that there were undisturbed old trees and underbrush growing before the bison arrived. In order to do the damage reported, bison had to have arrived no more than a few decades earlier. In Kentucky in the late 1700s, Daniel Boone's time, there were so few hunters that the game was fairly tame as well as abundant. Boone recounted in 1769 that one day he saw buffalo "numbering up in the thousands—at one lick a hundred acres were densely massed with these bulky animals, who exhibited no fear until the wind blew from the hunters toward them, and then they would dash wildly away in large droves and disappear."

In the West there was a similar surge of bison as in the East. It petered out in California's northeast Lassen County by 1830, and by 1855 there were no longer bison west of the front-range of the Rocky Mountains. The barriers keeping modern bison out of the Great Basin and the valleys of California appear to have been a combination of periodic accumulations of deep, wet snow, poor habitat, and hunting by Native Americans.

Bison were the only large grazing herbivores left after the extinctions at the end of the Ice Age, and as the Native North Americans' population declined in the 1600s, they made up in numbers what the plains lacked in faunal diversity. The retreating glaciers left much of the land covered with fertile silt and loess, while the Rocky Mountains, formed largely from old marine sediments, had weathered into nutrient-rich soil. The plains, when pelted by summer rains and watered by melting winter snows, were fertile and, in the absence of native hunters, they were teeming with life.

This abundance was described by such keen observers such as Prince Maximilian zu Wied and his illustrator Karl Bodmer during their travels up the Missouri River in 1833 to 1834, painter George Catlin's notes and letters published in 1841, and other eyewitness accounts. During their travels to the Pacific Coast, Meriwether Lewis and William Clark were constantly astonished at the massive bison herds they encountered; at the White River in the Dakotas in 1806, Lewis wrote in his *Journals* that "We discovered more [buffalo] than we had ever seen before at one time; and if it be not impossible to calculate the moving multitude, which darkened the whole plains, we are convinced that twenty thousand would be no exaggerated number." In 1849, historian Francis Parkman in *The Oregon Trail* described the sight: "The whole face of the country was dotted far and wide with countless hundreds of buffalo. They trooped along in files and columns, bulls, cows and calves, on the green faces of the declivities in front. They scrambled away over the hills to the right and left; and far off, the pale blue swells in the extreme distance were dotted with innumerable specks." Even William "Buffalo Bill" Cody recounted the glory days of his namesake animal in the mid-1800s: "The country was alive with buffaloes. Vast herds of these monarchs of the plains were roaming all around us."

Buffaloes and Wolves

In the heyday of the big bison herds on the open prairie, great wolf packs were their constant companions. The buffalo wolves were not the largest of the wolves, but not the smallest either. The majority were light gray, even white in color, with only a rare one in a black coat, a color not at all unusual in western gray wolves today. They congregated in large groups, with as many as seventy wolves to some packs. Due to their light coats they resembled flocks of sheep in the eye of George Catlin.

The bison herds appeared to pay little attention to these wolves, even when the wolves were in their midst. As early as 1811, explorer John Bradbury in the Dakotas noted this same bison behavior, writing in his journals: "We passed very close to several herds of buffaloe during the afternoon, near which we always observed a number of wolves lurking. I perceived that those herds which had wolves in their vicinity,

PAWNEE BUFFALO HEAD PICTOGRAPH
Painted in the center of a Pawnee shield made of cured buffalo rawhide, this effigy was then surrounded by eagle feathers. The shield's owner may have seen the buffalo spirit during a vision quest and invoked his guardian animal to protect him from danger.

Wolves are numerous and insolent.
—*Alexander Henry the Younger,*
Journals, *1799–1814*

"Slaughter of Buffaloes on the Plains"
Wolves and carrion birds gorge themselves on the remains of a human buffalo hunt in this drawing by Theodore R. Davis that appeared in Harper's Weekly *in 1872. (Courtesy of the Kansas State Historical Society)*

were almost wholly females with their calves; but noticed also, that there were always a few bulls with them, and that these were always stationed on the outside of the herd, inclosing the cows with their calves within."

How is it that a predator as thoroughly competent in killing bison as the wolf was tolerated, and apparently ignored, by buffalo herds at close range? Observing wolves and bison in Wood Buffalo National Park suggests that, contrary to appearance, bison pay close attention to wolves. Bison cows are sensitive to these predators, despite the fact that they act in a nonchalant fashion when wolves are around, even when there are wounded bison in the herd. Bison in Wood Buffalo are under so much pressure by wolves that about 1 percent of adults have lost their tails, and herds may run up to forty miles (64 km) nonstop to shake off pursuing wolves. And yet when a wolf shows up, the bison give every sign of ignoring it; when the wolf is gone, they leave.

While flight is undoubtedly effective in escaping wolves, it is also uses up a great deal of energy. A ruminant bison runs on a slim daily surplus of energy above maintenance requirements. This surplus it needs for growth, body repair, fattening, changing hair coats, and above all, for reproduction. Running costs are ten or more times maintenance costs and far exceed the rate of daily net energy gain under even optimal forage conditions. With many wolves about, a bison that spooks at wolves all the time would have to run nonstop and forego feeding. This cannot be. Consequently, bison have to be judicious about when to run and when to stay put and confront potential danger. There are many accounts by early European observers on the Great Plains of bison bulls who were unwilling to leave, were confrontational, were oblivious of danger from humans, and were generally acting "stupid." Canadian explorer David Thompson related in his journals of his travels in the West of 1784 to 1812 that some old plains bulls were at times quite bold and aggressive.

In confrontations with people, normally timid bison bulls could become dangerous when pursued and occasionally were reluctant to move from people on foot. Lone bulls in winter, in particular, were more likely to fight than run according to David Thompson, and bulls would often turn on horse and rider if they were tired from running or if they had been wounded. Hunters on foot found it important to lie down when close to bison and not move or bulls might become menacing. Francis Parkman reported that when a herd was chased by mounted men, the bulls dropped back so that the cows were in the vanguard. This may have been inadvertent as cows are better runners than bulls, but bulls have been seen placing themselves deliberately between cows with calves and wolves.

Adult bison are large animals and not at all easy to bring down, even for several wolves; a mature bison can trample on wolves and gore them with quick attacks and powerful thrusts of its horns. Group defense by bison was common when the great herds roamed the plains, and wolves following bison avoided attacking herds as these would quickly turn on them, noted Catlin. Instead, wolf packs waited for sick bison or bison wounded by hunters to fall behind the moving herd and delayed the attack as long as they and their victims were in sight of the herd. Bison attacked by wolves defended themselves vigorously and died a hard, lingering death. Catlin gives a vivid description of an old bull that was torn to pieces bit by bit as it stood its ground, and similar observations have been made in recent times by Dr. Carbyn. In the heyday of the herds, any bison carcass not claimed was likely to be devoured by wolves overnight, sometimes despite protective measures such as cloths left with the carcass by hunters to spook wolves with human scent. The sheer number of wolves on the prairie may have been a consequence of the many bison killed by hunters merely for their hides and tongues.

In Wood Buffalo National Park today, wolf packs appear to ignore sick, incapacitated adult bison, even ignoring carcasses of adults that have died from disease. They prefer to go after bison calves. Bison calves, smaller and hornless, are much less dangerous and are a better choice of prey than healthy adult bison; however, success is by no means assured because adult bison readily come to their defense. If cows with small calves are harassed by wolves and bull groups are around, the cows and calves may run into these groups for protection. Attacks on cows with calves by a wolf pack may last hours, but so may the spirited defenses by bulls.

The bulls not only continually maneuver so as to block wolves from calves, dash out to gore wolves, or sweep wolves off downed calves, but even close formation about calves while on the move. Observers in Wood Buffalo National Park photographed a running bull and cow close together with a calf in between—and a large wolf riding on the back of both adults. When large herds still roamed the prairie, Catlin noted that bison bulls would mingle with cows and their calves, as if protecting the latter. These bulls were hazardous to approach.

Cows that do not seek shelter within a group of bulls when confronted by a wolf

From Wakan Tanka, the Great Spirit, there came a great unifying life force that flowed in and through all things—the flowers of the plains, blowing winds, rocks, trees, birds, animals—and was the same force that had been breathed into the first man. Thus all things were kindred, and were brought together by the same Great Mystery. Kinship with all creatures of the earth, sky, and water was a real and active principle. In the animal and bird world there existed a brotherly feeling that kept the Lakota safe among them. And so close did some of the Lakotas come to their feathered and furred friends that in true brotherhood they spoke a common tongue. The animals had rights—the right of man's protection, the right to live, the right to multiply, the right to freedom, and the right to man's indebtedness—and in recognition of these rights the Lakota never enslaved an animal, and spared all life that was not needed for food and clothing.

—Oglala Sioux Chief Luther Standing Bear

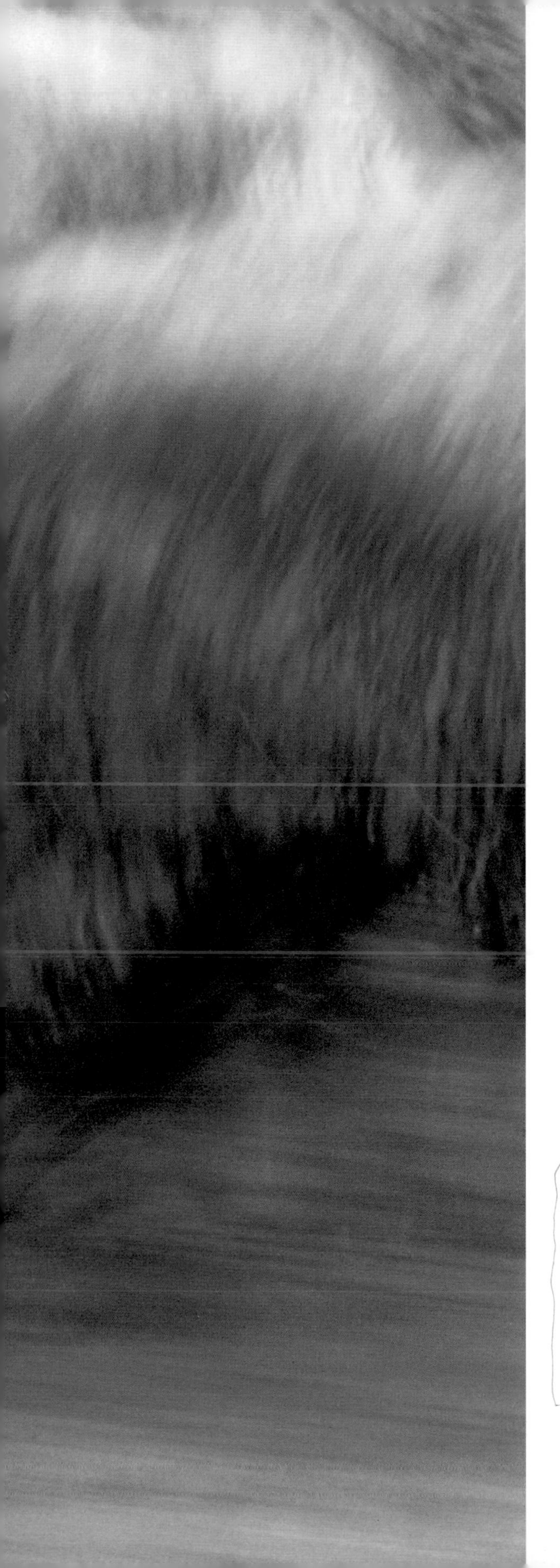

may elect to converge and form a loose assembly with the calves in the center. They do not form a dense ring of bodies, horns to the outside, as musk ox do. Young bulls accompanying the nursery herd periodically charge out at the wolf, which evades the attack and continues circling, inspecting the bison. The female bison act as if they are ignoring the wolf, which may lie down close to the herd. A peaceful idyll appears to form with the bison standing, resting, ruminating, or feeding. Nothing changes much after the wolf decides to leave. The bison carry on as if nothing matters. However, a half hour later, they are suddenly up and alert, and march off rapidly in single file. Should the wolf return with reinforcements, it will find the bison gone.

The days of the huge herds and the accompanying wolf packs on the Great Plains were numbered. For two centuries nature ran riot, amazing and confounding European observers, leaving the myth of nature's unending bounty and fixing the false modern image of pre-Columbian North America as a "natural paradise." Then, just as it was the absence of humans that gave rise to this intense flowering of nature, so it was their presence that put an abrupt end to it as the newly arrived European immigrants reduced the freedom of natural forces to operate.

RUNNING HERD
The high mobility of bison as well as the sudden appearance and disappearance of a herd were a cause of anxiety for the plains Indians, who subsisted on the animals. Consequently, when bison herds were close to a village it was left undisturbed and carefully watched over until a highly disciplined, large-scale hunt could be organized. (Photo © Layne Kennedy)

I entered into the Staked Plains and turned north. At some point in my journey it became clear to me that I was moving against the grain of time.

I came to a great canyon in the plain and descended into it. It was a very beautiful place. There was clear water and high green grass. A great herd of buffalo was grazing there. I moved slowly among those innumerable animals, coming so close to some that I could touch them, and I did touch them, and the long, dusty hair of their hides was crinkled and coarse in my fingers. In among them they were so many that I could not see the ground beneath them; they seemed a great, thick meadow of dark grain, and their breathing was like the sound of a huge, close swarm of bees. Guadal-tseyu and I, we picked our way, going very slowly, stitch by stitch—and otherwise they paid us no mind. We were a long time in their midst, it seemed a long time passing through. And farther on there were tipis, some of them partly dismantled, and little fires gone and going out, embers smoldering, and many things were strewn about, as if a people were breaking camp. But there were no people; the people had gone away. And for a long time after that I followed their tracks.

—*N. Scott Momaday,* The Names, *1976*

▲▲▲ Chapter 3 ▲▲▲

Extermination of the Bison

The civilization of the Indian is impossible while the buffalo remains upon the plains.
—Columbus Delano, U.S. Secretary of Interior, 1873

In 1889, an outraged U.S. National Museum zoologist by the name of William T. Hornaday published a call to arms concerning the fate of the buffalo. The article, entitled "The Extermination of the American Bison, with a Sketch of its Discovery and Life History," appeared in the *Report of the U.S. National Museum.* Concerned by the bison's decline but rather uncritical of the reasons for it, Hornaday blamed pitiless mass killing by Native Americans and greedy market hunters for bringing the buffalo to the brink of extinction. It is now difficult to comprehend how Hornaday could have missed what appears to be obvious even from his own account—that the extermination of the bison was an unspoken national policy of the United States government, and the hide and tongue hunters mere instruments of that policy.

KIOWA BUFFALO PICTOGRAPH
Painted on a tipi owned by Kiowa Never Got Shot, this buffalo bull with its red heartline was one of a herd of bison encircling the bottom of the tipi.

LONE BUFFALO
Pages 68–69, main photo: *A sole buffalo grazes amid the graceful ridges of Theodore Roosevelt National Park in North Dakota. (Photo © J. Ruggles)*

DAKOTA BUFFALO PICTOGRAPH
Page 69, inset: *A dramatic Dakota Sioux image of a running bison. Known as a "heartline," the arrow leading from the animal's mouth to its heart was originally painted in brilliant red.*

By the middle of the nineteenth century, Native North Americans on the Great Plains hunted bison primarily from horseback. Initially, native hunters used lances to spear individual buffalo, turning later to bows and arrows. Although some bows were strong enough to let loose arrows that killed the quarry, many wounded buffalo escaped only to be killed by wolves. The early black-powder guns traded to the Indians and half-breed Métis were not powerful by modern standards and were difficult to reload on horseback.

Chasing buffalo on horseback required organization and discipline. The aim was to make bison run in a circle, which allowed the riders to dispatch a large number of animals. William "Buffalo Bill" Cody described his hunting style as though it were his own in his *True Tales of the Plains* published in 1908: "My great forte in killing buffaloes from horseback was to get them circling by riding my horse at the head of the herd, shooting the leaders, thus crowding their followers to the left, till they would finally circle round and round." The chase on horseback was exciting but apparently posed little danger to an experienced hunter. Although some European sportsmen loved the chase, others thought little of it, and some even found hunting feral long-horned cattle in Texas more thrilling and dangerous.

The meat of choice from bison was the tongue and the fat anterior portions of the hump. For Native North Americans, the bone marrow and liver were also important. The liver was eaten raw, and at least one visiting sportsman developed a taste for it, as well as for raw brain. The preferred bison for the robe trade were young females. Native hunters tended to make fairly complete use of bison carcasses; European hunters often did not. Some, such as Francis Parkman, ran bison for sport and contented themselves with cutting off the tail of each bison killed—evidence of their success for the campfire bragging session.

The plains Indians' dependence on buffalo for everything from food to spiritual beliefs has become legend. But little has been written on the reliance of some European explorers and traders upon buffalo meat for their survival. In Major W. F. Butler's narrative of his travels across the Canadian plains in the mid-1800s, he describes the value of buffalo to the Europeans: "The meat, pounded down and mixed with fat into 'pemmican,' was found to supply a most excellent food for transport service, and accordingly vast numbers of buffalo were destroyed to supply the demand of the fur traders." Pemmican became a major source of food for fur traders and in one instance saved an early white settlement, that of the Selkirk settlers in the Canadian Red River valley who would have perished without the dried bison meat supplied them by the Métis.

It is doubtful that the way of life of the horse-mounted Native North Americans was ecologically sustainable in the long run. By the middle of the nineteenth century, bison were in decline from many factors, including overhunting, drought, and range and water competition from growing mustang and cattle herds. There was some respite for bison when smallpox, cholera, and intertribal warfare ravaged the Native North American population. Yet before the native horse culture, already tied to the continental trading network and exploiting bison for the robe trade, could

"LAST OF THE BUFFALO"
Above: *American painter Albert Bierstadt was famous for his golden-light, romantic vision of North America's grandeur, and this 1889 oil painting of an Indian spearing a gigantic buffalo bull certainly perpetuated his ideal. (Courtesy of the Buffalo Bill Historical Center, Cody, WY)*

WINTER STORM
Right: *A herd of bison weathers a winter storm sweeping across Wyoming. Severe winter storms may have been a blessing for buffalo when hard pressed by rising Indian populations in pre-Columbian times. Such storms made human life on the plains difficult, thus giving bison, deer, and elk temporary winter sanctuary. (Photo © Alan and Sandy Carey)*

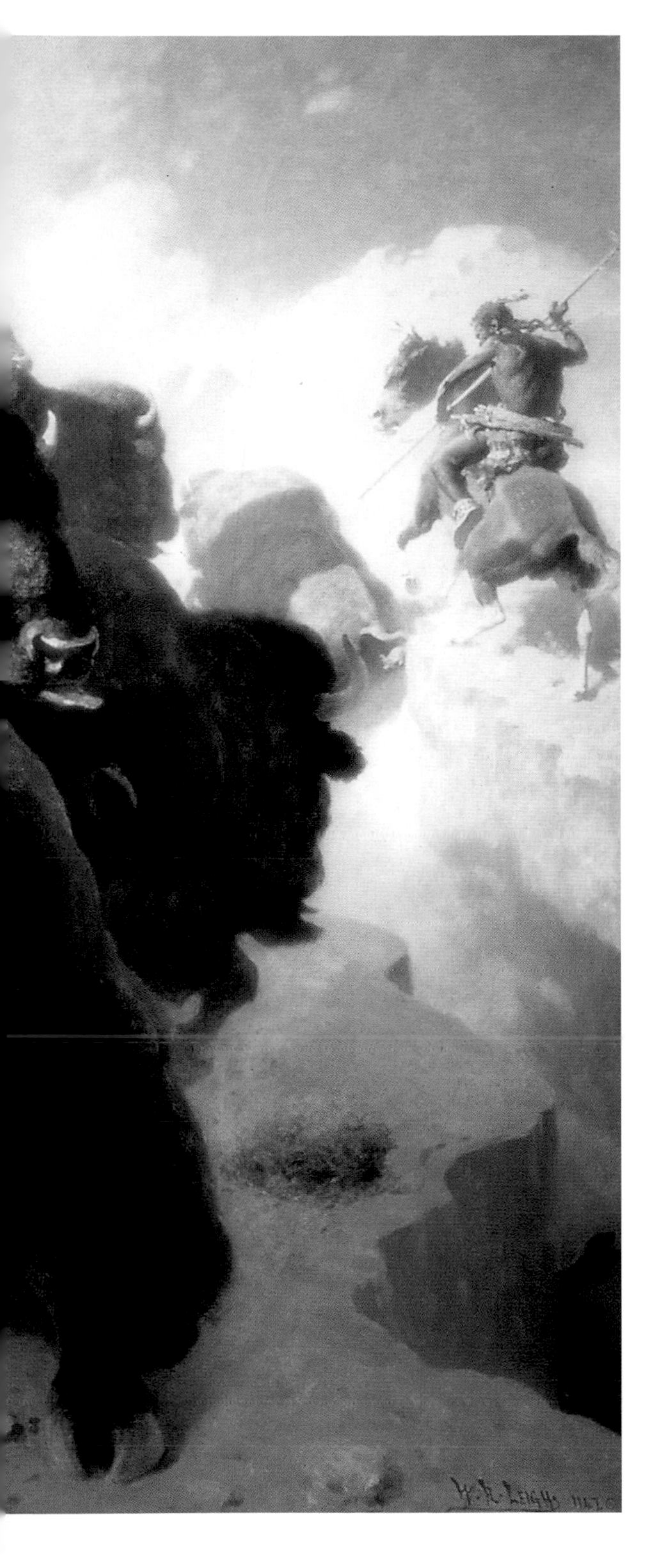

"An Assiniboine running a Buffalo"
Above: *This drawing was created "by an Assiniboine warrior and hunter. Fort Union. Jan. 16. 1854." (Courtesy of the National Anthropological Archives/Smithsonian Institution)*

"The Great Buffalo Hunt"
Left: *Horses arrived in North America with the Spanish conquistadors in the sixteenth century. Mounted on horseback, native hunters dramatically revised their buffalo-hunting strategies and no longer had to depend on difficult and laborious tactics of hunting buffalo on foot or with corrals. This oil painting by William Robinson Leigh was made in 1947 after the buffalo was largely extirpated and the Native North American horse culture destroyed. Leigh's dramatic vision was filled with nostalgia for days gone by. (Courtesy of the Rockwell Museum, Corning, NY)*

When I was at Washington the Great White Father told me that all the Comanche land was ours, and that no one should hinder us in living upon it. So, why do you ask us to leave the rivers, and the sun, and the wind, and live in houses? Do not ask us to give up the buffalo for the sheep.
—Parra-Wa-Samen (Ten Bears) of the Yamparika Comanche, 1872

BUFFALO HUNT PICTOGRAPH
This painted elk hide from the 1920s depicts a buffalo hunt surrounding an Indian village. Hides were painted both for decoration and as a record of a family's or tribe's history. This painting was created by artist Katsi Kodi, son of Charlie Washakie. (Courtesy of the Rockwell Museum, Corning, NY)

eliminate the herds, other factors conspired against them and the bison.

In The Way of Civilization

Legislation to save the buffalo was passed by a good margin by both houses of the U.S. Congress on June 23, 1874, but died for lack of a presidential signature. In truth, the bill had no hope of passage or effective implementation from the outset. The president who let the legislation die by pigeon-holing it was the former commander of the Union armies during the Civil War, Ulysses S. Grant.

Of the many forces aligned against the bison at the time, the foremost was the United States Army, particularly the Military Department of the Southwest commanded by General Philip H. Sheridan and the Army of the Missouri commanded by General William Tecumseh Sherman. Clearly, President Grant, their former commander, colleague, and promoter during the Civil War, was not about to approve legislation that flew in the face of the policy his fellow officers and friends had been implementing for over five years.

After the Civil War, the Native Americans living on the Great Plains stood squarely—and effectively—in the way of ongoing U.S. expansion into the West. Pressure was building. For decades Native Americans had skirmished with mountain men who trapped for beavers and other pelts in the West. Jedediah Smith had crossed from the Great Basin to California by 1826; Captain Joe Walker pioneered better routes by 1834; settlers crossed the plains to Oregon and the Great Basin in the 1840s; and the California Gold Rush drew large numbers of adventurers across the Great Plains by the late 1840s. Native Americans knew by then that smallpox was infectious and were uneasy about contact; Army Captain Howard Stanbury told of Oglala Sioux in 1850 hesitating to approach his party because they feared the soldiers bore smallpox, which they claimed was raging close to Fort Laramie and from which they had fled.

Although the native horsemen—primarily the Apaches, Comanches, and Kiowas—had kept the Spaniards from spreading into the Great Plains for nearly two centuries, by 1800 a number of developments had taken place. Firearms had been perfected beyond anything the Spaniards could ever have dreamt of possessing; buffalo robes and hides were popular items in the East and Europe; by 1835, steamships were ascending the large rivers and could bring the products to market; and by 1865 railways were moving into the West. In short, the means were becoming available to exploit bison as a resource. The plunder of North America's wildlife had commenced and was about to drive that wildlife to near extinction.

By the mid-1800s, Native Americans and bison were seen by European settlers as standing in the way of "civilization." Even before the Civil War, cattle herds were driven from Texas through Kansas and came to grief upon meeting herds of bison; thus bison were viewed as an impediment to cattle ranching. In 1860, the Pony Express was organized, cutting across the Great Plains from St. Joseph, Missouri, to Sacramento, California. By 1867, the Kansas Pacific Railway reached the center of the bison range, bringing more settlers as well as buffalo hunters including William "Buffalo Bill" Cody, who was hired by the railroad to kill buffalo to feed

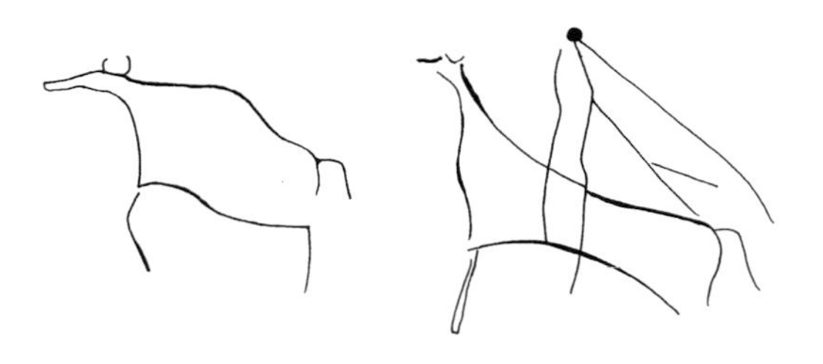

BUFFALO HUNT PETROGLYPH
A hunter on horseback pursues a buffalo in this image carved into rock at Writing-on-Stone, Alberta.

A Tourist in Buffalo Land

Manifest Destiny brought not only the Army and settlers to the West, but also tourists. W. E. Webb of Topeka, Kansas, went west by railroad in the late 1800s to gawk at buffalo and Indians, and to hunt with Buffalo Bill as his guide. His 1872 account of these travels, *Buffalo Land: An Authentic Account of the Discoveries, Adventures, and Mishaps of a Scientific and Sporting Party with Graphic Descriptions of the Country; the Red Man, Savage and Civilized; Hunting the Buffalo, Antelope, Elk, and Wild Turkey, etc., etc. Replete with Information, Wit, and Humor*, offers rare insight into the thinking of at least one early European-American: An intensely racist attitude towards "civilizing" the Indians by any means and joyous pleasure at the westward march of progress—all expressed in an oddly poetic spirit.

Gathering twilight had magnified what in broad day would have been an apparition startling to any new arrival in Buffalo Land. A long line of black, shaggy forms was standing on the crest and looking down upon us. It had come forward like the rush of a hungry wave, and now remained as one uplifted, dark and motionless. In bold relief against the horizon stood an array of colossal figures, all bristling with sharp points, which at first sight seemed lances, but at second resolved into horns. Then it dawned upon our minds that a herd of great American bison stood before us. What a grateful reduction of lumps in more than one throat, and how the air ran riot in lately congealed lungs!

One old fellow, evidently a leader in Buffalo Land, with long patriarchal beard and shaggy forehead, remained in front, his head upraised. His whole attitude bespoke intense astonishment. For years this had been their favorite path between Arkansas and the Platte. Big Creek's green valley had given succulent grasses to old and young of the bison tribe from time immemorial. Every hollow had its traditions of fierce wolf fights and Indian ambuscades, and many a stout bull could remember the exact spot where his charge had rescued a mother and her young from the hungry teeth of starving timber wolves. Every wallow, tree, and sheltering ravine were sacred in the traditions of Buffalo Land. The petrified bones of ancestors who fell to sleep there a thousand years before testified to purity of bison blood and pedigree.

Now all this was changed. Rushing toward their loved valley, they found themselves in the suburbs of a town. Yells of red man and wolf were never so horrible as that of the demon flashing along the valley's bed. A great iron path lay at their feet, barring them back into the wilderness. Slowly the shaggy monarch shook his head, as if in doubt whether this was a vision or not; then whirling suddenly, perhaps indignantly, he turned away and disappeared behind the ridge, and the bison multitude followed.

"A Herd of Buffalo and a U.P. Train" painting by Walter Lockhart, 1931
Above: *(Courtesy of the Kansas State Historical Society)*

Buffalo Land
Right: *Title page of* W. E. Webb's *bizarre chronicle of his tour of the once-wild west, published in 1872.*

"WHEN THE LAND BELONGED TO GOD"
A romantic depiction of a time gone by: A herd of buffalo crosses the Missouri River without a human being in sight. This image was painted in oil in 1914 by famed Montana cowboy painter Charles M. Russell; his trademark signature with buffalo skull is in the lower left corner. (Courtesy of the Montana State Historical Society)

the tracklayers.

The bison slaughter distressed the Native Americans. Naturally, they opposed Manifest Destiny as perceived by the American populous, who in turn believed that the Indians had to be eliminated as an obstacle to progress. While the United States Army was under political pressure in the West to do something about the Indian menace, the Native Americans' goal was to keep competitors off the buffalo range. As Cheyenne Chief Roman Nose said at a council between U.S. General Palmer and Cheyenne chiefs near Fort Ellsworth, Kansas, in 1866, "We will not have the wagons which make a noise [steam locomotives] in the hunting grounds of the buffalo. If the palefaces come farther into our land, there will be scalps of your brethern in the wigwams of the Cheyenne. I have spoken."

The pressure the Native American warriors brought to bear on the settlers came as swift, unpredictable raids that killed some settlers or soldiers; tortured others; whisked women and children into captivity; and left buildings, stores, and equipment burning and livestock killed, stolen, or scattered. Such tactics had worked well for over two centuries in stopping advances by the Spaniards, and continued to be effective against the white people's manifest destiny. Settlers hated Indians not only because of the losses and personal grief inflicted on them, but—and this must have been most aggravating—because measures to counter the Indian raids proved largely ineffective. Despite propaganda to the contrary, the army and settlers were being outfought and outgeneraled. A handful of clever and competent nomad-warriors using guerrilla tactics were defying a proud, victorious, modern, and well-equipped army. Generals Sherman and Sheridan faced no small problem.

With the wisdom of hindsight it is little wonder the Native Americans were so successful against the army. A good many of the soldiers were recent immigrants from

BUFFALO STAMPEDE
Overleaf: *A herd of bison on the run. Early explorers tell that wary buffalo herds would dash away in a panic upon smelling the unfamiliar scent of white men. (Photo © Michael H. Francis)*

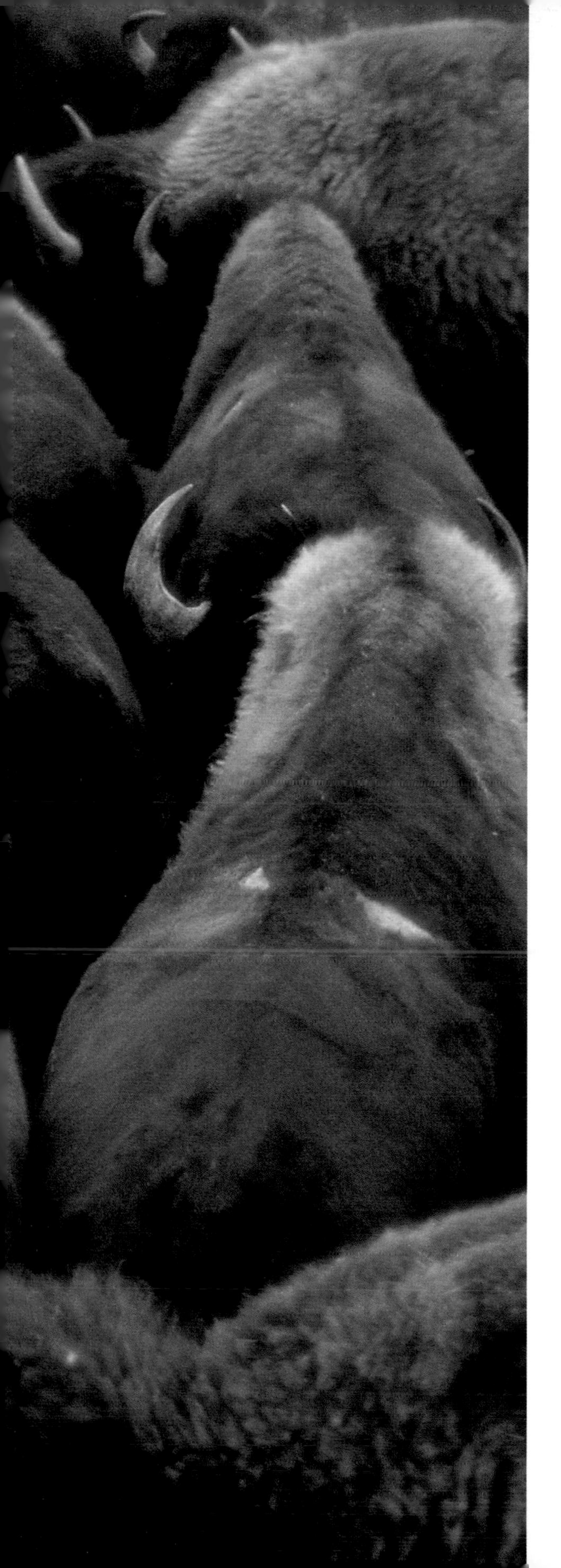

The Business of Buffalo Hunting

Buffalo hunting was big business on the great plains by the mid-1800s. The following collection of first-hand accounts tells something of the life of the buffalo hunters:

THE NEXT DAY we came across the buffalo herd, a small one, and each man that had a buffalo horse—that is, a fast runner, one that can run a half-mile a minute—got on its back and chased buffalo. There were fifty or sixty in the herd, and out of these we killed forty-five. We used single and double-barreled guns, and loaded our guns as we rode. We skinned the buffalo, cut up the meat and packed it in our carts. I was delighted, as this was my first buffalo hunt.
—Buffalo hunter Norbert Welsh, as told to Mary Weekes, *The Last Buffalo Hunter*, 1939

MY NEXT EXPERIENCE with buffaloes and hunters, etc., was in the late fall of 1871. Many more people took to the killing of buffalos for the meat, which they dried, but mostly for the skins.

There was a little village started on Turkey creek about 16 miles North and some west of the new Medicine Lodge town.

Some of the hunters had made a number of rooms (homes) side by side by cutting spaces in the creek bank (east side). They placed logs overhead, then brush and dirt; also sods on top to a level with the rest of the land. No buffalo could ever guess that there was any human around, and they would come sometimes right over to their habitations, and about.

Those people would kill them, take the skins and the very finest part of the meat to dry for the Hutchinson market. They placed poison on the rest for the gray wolves and cayotes [*sic*] who had become very plentifull [*sic*] in that land of their plentifull food. And the first thing after breakfast the hunters did was to go to their job of skinning wolves. Any newcomers would have been astonished at the amount of buffalo and wolf carcasses laying around in that neighborhood.
—L. C. Fouquet, *Buffalo Days*, 1871

THE BUFFALOES CAME rushing past me not a hundred yards distant. . . . Now, thought I, is the time to "get my work in," as they say; and I pulled the blind-bridle from my horse, who knew as well as I did that we were out for buffaloes—as he was a trained hunter. The moment the bridle was off, he started at the top of his speed . . . and with a few jumps he brought me alongside of the rear buffalo. Raising old "Lucretia Borgia" to my shoulder, I fired, and killed the animal at the first shot.
—William "Buffalo Bill" Cody, *Story of the Wild West and Camp-Fire Chats*, 1888

A FEW WEEKS later we started on a winter hunt, just the men. A party of ten men started out on our buffalo runners. A blinding blizzard came on. It was about forty below zero, but we kept on. I shot ten buffalo. Then we had to skin the buffalo in the blizzard. We were on the open plain, and had no shelter, but we were not cold. We were no weaklings, we men of the old brigades! I had a man helping me. The first cow we skinned, we cut her open, and to pieces. Then I cut a hole in the tripe. The manure was hot, and whenever our hands got cold, we would run and put them in the manure, and they would be as warm as fire.
—Buffalo hunter Norbert Welsh, as told to Mary Weekes, *The Last Buffalo Hunter*, 1939

IT WAS AGREED that each [of his party of eight] should select his buffalo, and a charge was ordered. It was not long before the herd was on the move, and a wild scene presented itself. The herd scattered in every direction. Bang, bang, in every direction could be heard. It was not long before everything was still but the whistling north wind. . . .
—Captain William Banta, *Twenty-Seven Years on the Texas Frontier*, 1870

MOUND OF BUFFALO SKULLS

A pile of bison skulls in 1880 towers more than fifty feet (15 m) in the air above a worker at the Michigan Carbon Works in Detroit where the bones were to be processed for industrial use. (Courtesy of the Detroit Public Library)

In my youthful days, I have seen large herds of buffalo on these prairies, and elk were found in every grove, but they are here no more, having gone towards the setting sun. For hundreds of miles no white man lived, but now trading posts and settlers are found here and there throughout the country, and in a few years the smoke from their cabins will be seen to ascend from every grove, and the prairie covered with their cornfields.

—*Potawatomi Chief Sabonee, 1827*

Europe who were undernourished and in poor health; the Native Americans were well fed, large, and strong. The U.S. soldiers were poorly trained whereas the native men were schooled to be warriors and hunters: how to handle horses, how to stalk enemies, how to use weapons, how to perform ruses and deceptions, how to fight at close quarters—all this was second nature to Native American boys growing into men. The soldiers, meanwhile, often deserted the unbearable conditions on the frontier; Native American warriors were fighting on their home ground and knew the Great Plains intimately. Moreover, the Native Americans were well motivated: They were fighting for their freedom against an enemy in whose word, experience had taught them, they could place little trust. They knew only too well the conditions on the reservations, and that deprivation, disease, and hunger awaited them.

The mounted Indian warriors could not be subdued by conventional military means, despite the army's best efforts. General George Armstrong Custer's hapless escapades in Indian Territory in 1867 were followed in 1868 by the humiliating defeat and withdrawal of the U.S. Army from the Powder River and the abandonment of its forts. This terminated "Red Cloud's War," two years of effective resistance by the Sioux and Cheyenne to the U.S. Army's effort to secure the Bozeman Trail through Wyoming to the goldfields in Montana. The Native Americans judiciously avoided engagements that favored the Army and struck in sophisticated raids that invariably caught the soldiers, settlers, and buffalo hunters at a disadvantage.

Native warriors rarely suffered serious setbacks. Defeats came only when they attacked entrenched troops or buffalo hunters: Consider the Battle of Adobe Walls in June 1874, when a force of some seven hundred Comanche and Kiowa under Chief Quanah Parker attacked a group of twenty-eight buffalo hunters barricaded within a solid building, and only the marksmanship of the hunters got the better of the warriors. Defeats also came when army troops were able to surprise small native settlements. There are many examples on record of advantages gained by the army in finding and destroying Indian encampments; however, an attack on an Indian encampment also led to the U.S. Army's greatest defeat in Custer's Last Stand. The Native Americans won big results for limited effort. It was simply good generalship.

JEMEZ PUEBLO BISON-HIDE SHIELD

This shield made of tanned bison hide was painted with a dramatic image of a bison head, invoking the animal's powerful spirit to serve as protection. (Courtesy of the Denver Museum of Natural History)

The War on the Buffalo

When an enemy is not readily defeatable in battle, however, one can still subdue it by destroying its basis of operations, its supplies, its economic lifeline. The Indian tribes of the West were completely dependent on the bison—which was a liability, even though bison were quite numerous after the Civil War. None other than General George Armstrong Custer summed it up best in his *Wild Life on the Plains*, published posthumously in 1891, reported one key reason that the U.S. Army was at that

William "Buffalo Bill" Cody

Across the rolling, trackless plains
I see a vision as of old.
Aye, like a knight in armor girt,
As noble, free and quite as bold;
His flowing locks and massive brow
Proclaimed the gallant life he passed
While toiling to prepare the way
For those who built an empire vast.
They called him Bill—
Just Buffalo Bill.
—F. P. Livingston, "The Great Scout," 1927

Looking back from today's vantage it is almost impossible to separate the man who was William F. Cody from the legend that was Buffalo Bill. Cody was an Indian killer and a buffalo hunter, occupations that crowned him a hero in the late 1800s but today tarnish his fame with infamy. He was a creation of the American West—and in turn played a key role in defining our latter-day vision of the Wild West.

Cody was born in LeClaire, Iowa, on February 26, 1846. He quit school early to work as a bullwhacker for a freight company. He moved on to pan for gold in Colorado by the age of thirteen. At the ripe age of fourteen, he was a Pony Express rider, for which he won renown as a fearless, enduring long-distance rider and had his first skirmishes with Indians. He served in the Kansas Cavalry during the Civil War and after the war, as a scout with the U.S. Army, fighting the Sioux.

In 1867, he was hired by the Kansas Pacific Railroad (later known as the Union Pacific) to kill buffalo to feed tracklayers. He recounted these exploits in one of his several popular biographies, *Story of the Wild West and Camp-Fire Chats*, published in 1888:

THE CONSTRUCTION OF the end of the track got into the great buffalo country, and at that time the Indians—the Sioux, Cheyennes, Comanches, and Arapahoes—were all on the war-path. It was before the refrigerator car was in use and the contractors had no fresh meat to feed their employees. . . . I immediately began my career as a buffalo hunter for the Kansas Pacific Railroad, and it was not long before I acquired considerable notoriety. It was at this time that the very appropriate name of 'Buffalo Bill' was conferred upon me by the railhands. It has stuck to me ever since, and I have never been ashamed of it. During my engagement as hunter for the company—a period of less than eighteen months—I killed 4,280 buffaloes.

Cody cut a dashing figure with his flowing blond mane and fringed buckskin outfits, becoming the ideal of the frontiersmen conquering the Wild West by six-shooter and Winchester rifle. In 1869, dime-novel writer Ned Buntline, the pseudonym of Edward Judson, immortalized Buffalo Bill as a hero, and Cody subsequently starred in hundreds of novels and movies.

In 1872, Cody moved to Chicago to star in a dramatization of Buntline's novel. This new theatrical life tied in well with his past dramas, and he created his Wild West Show. As he told the tale in *Story of the Wild West*, "Immense success and comparative wealth, attained in the profession of showman, stimulated me to greater exertion and largely increased my ambition for public favor. Accordingly, I conceived the idea of organizing a large company of Indians, cowboys, Mexican vaqueros, famous riders and expert lasso throwers, with accessories of stage coach, emigrant wagons, bucking horses and a herd of buffaloes, with which to give a realistic entertainment of wild life on the plains."

The Wild West Show delighted eastern United States and European audiences, appearing in London in 1887 for Queen Victoria's Jubilee, and including "stars" such as Annie Oakley and Sitting Bull. A London newspaper's review of the show in 1882 captured the times and the realism of Cody's menagerie:

AS WE TOOK our places in one of the little boxes which edge the arena in the grounds of the American Exhibition where Buffalo Bill's Wild West Show is given, we could not help being struck with the effectiveness of the scene before us. There were the various tribes of Indians in their war-paint and feathers, the Mexicans, the ladies, and the cowboys, and a fine array they made, with the chiefs of each tribe, and the celebrated Buffalo Bill. . . . The buffalo hunt was immensely realistic. . . . Summing up the Wild

West Show, we would suggest for consideration the advantage of the introduction of a little scalping. Why should not the Indians overcome a party of scouts, and "raise their hair?"

In his later years, Buffalo Bill founded the town of Cody, Wyoming, and started efforts to preserve the namesake animal he was famous for hunting. When he died on January 10, 1917, more than 25,000 people filed past his casket, and President Theodore Roosevelt eulogized him as "one of those men, steel-thewed and iron-nerved, whose daring progress opened the great West to settlement and civilization."

BUFFALO BILL ADVERTISEMENT
Opposite: *A buffalo-head advertisement booklet for Buffalo Bill's Wild West and Congress of Rough Riders of the World. (Courtesy of the Buffalo Bill Historical Center, Cody, WY)*

BUFFALO BILL POSTER
Above: *An advertising poster announcing the arrival of the Buffalo Bill and Pawnee Bill Show featuring Rose Wentworth-Carr in a chariot pulled by her "Drove of Bucking and Racing Buffalo." (Courtesy of Circus World Museum, Baraboo, WI)*

We did not ask you white men to come here. The Great Spirit gave us this country as a home. You had yours. We did not interfere with you. The Great Spirit gave us plenty of land to live on, and buffalo, deer, antelope and other game. But you came here; you are taking my land from me; you are killing off our game, so it is hard for us to live. Now, you tell us to work for a living, but the Great Spirit did not make us to work, but to live by hunting. You white men can work if you want to. We do not interfere with you, and again you say, why do you not become civilized? We do not want your civilization! We would live as our fathers did, and their fathers before them.
—*Oglala Sioux Chief Crazy Horse, 1870s*

"Indian Hunting Buffalo"
A drawing by Felix O. C. Darley from 1844. (Courtesy of the Kansas State Historical Society)

time losing the war against the Indians: "The immense herds of buffalo and other varieties of game roaming undisturbed over the Plains supplied all the food that was necessary to subsist the war parties, and at the same time allow their villages to move freely from point to point. . . ." Extermination of the bison would mean the economic end for Indian people of the Great Plains. So the bison was slated for extermination.

The call to wage war on the bison echoed through the army and the U.S. Congress. In 1873, President Grant's Interior Secretary, Columbus Delano, succinctly outlined the government's unwritten philosophy: "The civilization of the Indian is impossible while the buffalo remains upon the plains." This sentiment was further propounded by Representative James Throckmorton of Texas in 1876: "There is no question that, so long as there are millions of buffaloes in the West, so long the Indians cannot be controlled, even by the strong arm of the Government. I believe it would be a great step forward in the civilization of the Indians and the preservation of peace on the border if there was not a buffalo in existence."

The idea to subdue the Indian tribes by eliminating the buffalo was not original; Sheridan and Sherman practiced a similar "scorched earth" policy on General Robert E. Lee's Confederate Army late in the Civil War. It had the desired results, but Sherman's and Sheridan's march through Georgia left more than fame for the Union general and scorched earth for the Confederacy: It left deep, abiding resentment in the South at the sheer brutality and ruthlessness of the campaign. Thus when Sherman and Sheridan moved west after the Civil War, they were already hated by Texans. Their anti-Indian policies would soon make heroes of them.

All that was required to neutralize the "Indian menace" was to organize effectively the factors that would destroy the bison. This would soon eliminate the Native Americans' ability to resist. The U.S. government and its army waged a covert war on Native Americans and the bison by employing a secret army of buffalo hunters. The government simply had to protect the hunters and insure that their lines of supply were secure.

Hide hunters were a serious and destructive lot, and they came with commerce in mind. Buffalo hides were very "plastic" and served primarily to provide the leather for belts to drive machinery in the burgeoning factories of the East. Buffalo robes were also much in demand for heavy winter coats as well as for their "Indian appeal."

Total War on the Buffalo

The U.S. government's campaign to exterminate the buffalo in the mid- to late 1800s was part of a "total war" to drive Native Americans onto reservations and open up the West for settlement and civilization. The following collection of quotes and excerpts outlines the philosophy behind the government and the Army's "scorched earth" war on the Native American and the buffalo:

We had crossed weapons with the Indians time and again during the mild summer months, when the rich verdure of the valleys served as bountiful and inexhaustible granaries in supplying forage to their ponies, and the immense herds of buffalo and other varieties of game roaming undisturbed over the Plains supplied all the food that was necessary to subsist the war parties, and at the same time allow their villages to move freely from point to point; and the experience of both officers and men went to prove that in attempting to fight Indians in the summer season we were yielding to them the advantages of climate and supplies—we were meeting them on ground of their own selection, and at a time when every natural circumstance controlling the result of a campaign was wholly in their favor; and as a just consequence the troops, in nearly all these contests with the red men, had come off second best.
—General George Armstrong Custer, *Wild Life on the Plains*, 1891

I would not seriously regret the total disappearance of the buffalo from our western plains, in its effect upon the Indians. I would regard it rather as a means of hastening their sense of dependence upon the products of the soil and their own labors.
—U.S. Secretary of the Interior Columbus Delano, 1873

The Texas Legislature, while we were here among the herds, to destroy them, was in session at Austin, with a bill drawn up for their protection. General Phil. Sheridan was then in command of the military department of the Southwest, with headquarters at San Antonio. When he heard of the nature of the Texas bill for the protection of the buffaloes, he went to Austin, and, appearing before the joint assembly of the House and Senate, so the story goes, told them that they were making a sentimental mistake by legislating in the interest of the buffalo. He told them that instead of stopping the hunters they ought to give them a hearty, unanimous vote of thanks, and appropriate a sufficient sum of money to strike and present to each one a medal of bronze, with a dead buffalo on one side and a discouraged Indian on the other. . . . His words had the desired effect, and for the next three years the American bison traveled through a hail of lead.
—John R. Cook, *The Border and the Buffalo*, 1875

Invite all the sportsmen of England and America this fall for a Great Buffalo Hunt and make a grand sweep of them all.
—Letter from General William Sherman, commander of the Army in the Sioux territory, to General Philip Sheridan

And at times I asked myself: "What would you do, John R. Cook, if you had been a child of this wonderfully prolific game region, your ancestors, back through countless ages, according to traditional history, having roamed these vast solitudes as free as the air they breathed? What would you do if some outside interloper should come in and start a ruthless slaughter upon the very soil you had grown from childhood upon, and that you believed you alone had all the rights by occupancy that could possibly be given one? Yes, what would you do?"

But there are two sides to the question. It is simply a case of the survival of the fittest. Too late to stop and moralize now. And sentiment must have no part in our thoughts from this time on. We must have these 3361 hides that this region is to and did furnish us inside of three months, within a radius of eight miles from this main camp. So at it we went. . . . It's simply a case of the survival of the fittest.
—John R. Cook, *The Border and the Buffalo*, 1875

In consideration of the advantages and benefits conferred by this treaty, and the many pledges of friendship by the United States, the tribes who are parties to this agreement hereby stipulate that they will relinquish all right to occupy permanently the territory outside their reservation as herein defined, but yet reserve the right to hunt on any lands north of North Platte, and on the Republican Fork of the Smoky Hill River, so long as the buffalo may range thereon in such numbers as to justify the chase.
—Article 11, Treaty of 1868 establishing the Great Sioux reservation

Ten years ago the Plains Indians had an ample supply of food. . . . Now everything is gone, and they are reduced to the condition of paupers, without food, shelter, clothing, or any of those necessaries of life which came from the buffalo.
—Colonel Richard Dodge, Indian fighter, 1882

You people make a big talk, and sometimes war, if an Indian kills a white man's ox to keep his wife and children from starving. What do you think my people ought to say and do when they themselves see their cattle [buffalo] killed by your race when they are not hungry?

—Cheyenne Chief Little Robe during a visit to Washington, D.C., 1870s

BLOOD INDIAN SHIELD

Adorned with a painting of a buffalo in its center, this shield was surrounded by owl, pheasant, and eagle feathers. (H65.263.1; Provincial Museum of Alberta, Edmonton, Canada)

"Hunting the Buffaloe"
The image of the noble Indian stalking the buffalo was one of beauty to many Europeans in the mid-1800s. Swiss artist Peter Rindesbacher painted this watercolor glorifying the Great Hunt. (Courtesy of the National Anthropological Archives/ Smithsonian Institution)

The hide hunters were also organized and effective. The main method of hunting was now long-range shooting with powerful breech-loading guns using meticulously hand-loaded ammunition. The aim was to get close to an unsuspecting bison herd and with carefully placed shots bag as many bison as possible, occasionally the whole herd. In 1882, an Indian agent at Fort Peck told of the buffalo hunters' tactics: "They used the high-powered long-range rifles which were effective at a range of perhaps a mile and a half. Equipped with these guns, the hunters would sight a herd of buffalo from a great distance and kill the leaders; then the herd, instead of stampeding, would 'mill' and the hunters would be able to kill the whole herd. By this method great numbers of these animals were slain in a remarkably short period of time. There is testimony in the records that one white hunter killed 6,200 buffalo in this territory in the winter of 1880." While the agent's account of the rifles' range is exaggerated, the guns were certainly effective. The bison were then skinned by helpers and the hides prepared for transport, while the rest usually remained untouched. Some hunters salted or smoked the tongue of buffalo to be sold as a delicacy. Native North Americans naturally despised and resented such hunting practices as a desecration of their spiritual animal; Canadian Assiniboine Chief Dan

PLAINS CREE AMULET
Above: *This amulet features a piece of ammonite, also known as buffalo stone, wrapped in heavily ochred bison hide and decorated with flicker feathers. This amulet was believed to have been owned by Plains Cree Chief Poundmaker, famous for his part in the bloody second Riel Rebellion against reservation life. According to family tradition, it was given to him by the Buffalo-That-Walks-Like-A-Man spirit in the Cypress Hills, and it helped the owner find buffalo. (H88.94.143; Provincial Museum of Alberta, Edmonton, Canada)*

WATERING HOLE
Right: *A herd of buffalo waters along the Firehole River in fall in Yellowstone National Park. Bison visited watering places on a regular daily basis and at these watering holes the early explorers, using guns of inferior range and killing power, would wait in ambush for herds. (Photo © Erwin and Peggy Bauer)*

BLOOD INDIAN LEDGER PAINTING
Native artisans sometimes used the backs of ledgers for drawings and paintings. This ledger painting showing a buffalo hunt was done between 1888 and 1902 and acquired by Charles McAnally, a teacher at St. Mary's school on the Blood reserve in Alberta. (H69.187.71; Provincial Museum of Alberta, Edmonton, Canada)

We cannot dwell side by side. Only seven years ago we made a treaty by which we were assured that the buffalo country should be left to us forever. Now they threaten to take that away from us. My brothers, shall we submit or shall we say to them: "First kill me before you take possession of my Fatherland."
—Hunkpapa Sioux Chief Sitting Bull speaking at a Powder River council, 1877

Kennedy (Ochankugahe) remembered acres and acres of dead buffalo when he was a child, the carcasses so close together he could walk across the prairie jumping from buffalo to buffalo.

For their part, the army ensured a safe haven for the hunters where they needed it most—along the railways. The army also provided supplies, as buffalo hunter Frank H. Mayer recounted: "The army officers in charge of plains operations encouraged the slaughter of buffalo in every possible way. Part of this encouragement was of a practical nature that we runners appreciated. It consisted of ammunition, free ammunition, all you could use, all you wanted, more than you needed. All you had to do to get it was apply at any frontier army post and say you were short of ammunition, and plenty would be given you. I received thousands of rounds this way."

From the army's standpoint, this strategy was a great success. In 1875, when the Texas Legislature contemplated protecting the last remnants of bison, General Philip Sheridan traveled to address a joint assembly of the House and Senate to dissuade them from passing the bill. He eulogized the hide hunters as national heroes deserving a vote of thanks and a medal: "These men have done in the last two years and will do more in the next year to settle the vexed Indian question, than the entire regular army has done in the last thirty years. They are destroying the Indian's commissary, and it is a well-known fact that an army losing its base of supplies is placed at a great disadvantage. Send them powder and lead, if you will; for the sake of lasting peace, let them kill, skin and sell until the buffaloes are exterminated. Then your prairies can be covered with speckled cattle and the festive cowboy, who follows the hunter as a second forerunner of an advanced civilization." The Texas bill never passed.

It took from about 1868 to 1883, or some fifteen years, to kill off the buffalo. Market hunting destroyed the southern herds by 1875; plains bison were virtually exterminated in the wild by early 1883. The last commercial shipment of hides was in 1889. By 1894, the only free-living bison remaining in the United States were found in Yellowstone National Park. Six years later, by 1902, this last wild herd was reduced by poachers to twenty-three animals.

However, helping to exterminate the bison was not the only tactic the U.S. Army employed in its war against the Indians. It also began to hunt down Native Americans in encampments, killing and dispersing the inhabitants and their horses, and burning food stores. Again, it was a "total war" campaign aimed against the native "hinterland," for warriors concerned about their families, deprived of horses and food, were not likely to fight effectively and might be demoralized enough to surrender to reservation life. General George Armstrong Custer's fame—if one can call it such—as an Indian fighter rested on this strategy, as he destroyed in November 1868 Cheyenne Chief Black Kettle's sleeping village on the Washita River. Colonel Nelson Miles used that strategy in his relentless pursuit of Sitting Bull's Hunkpapa Sioux following Custer's defeat at the Battle of the Little Bighorn.

The strategy was also used by the capable, hard Colonel Ronald S. Mackenzie, who eliminated the Comanches and

BUFFALO HIDE COAT
Articles made of buffalo became the rage of style in the United States and Canada in the late 1800s. This long buffalo hide coat was sold by the famous Hudson Bay Company. (Courtesy of the Buffalo Bill Historical Center, Cody, WY)

Only a few pieces from a young bull, and its tongue, were brought on board, most of the men being too lazy, or too far off, to cut out even the tongues of the others; and thus it is that thousands multiplied by thousands of Buffaloes are murdered in senseless play, and their enormous carcasses are suffered to be the prey of the Wolf, the Raven and the Buzzard, or to rot on the spots where they fell. The prairies were literally covered with the skulls of victims.

—*John James Audubon,* The Missouri River Journals, *1843*

On the move

Trailing a long plume of dust, a bison herd comes over the crest of a hill in Yellowstone National Park. Buffalo live in a dusty environment, and their large grinding teeth are in good part an adaptation to the terrible wear their teeth are subjected to from dust-coated vegetation. (Photo © Erwin and Peggy Bauer)

You can expect nothing whatsoever from the Queen's government except protection so long as you behave yourselves. Your only hope are the buffalo, and it will not be many years before that source of supply will cease.
—*Royal Canadian Mounted Police Commissioner James MacLeod in response to Sitting Bull's request for a Canadian reservation for his group of exiled Sioux, 1877*

Kiowas as an effective fighting force by late 1874. Mackenzie scattered a large encampment in the Palo Duro Canyon of Texas, shot some 1,400 captured Indian horses, and burned all tipis and supplies. By 1874, however, the food source of the Comanches, the great southern buffalo herd, was also largely history. Had bison still been numerous on the Texas uplands, had the dismounted Comanche and Kiowa warriors run into sizable herds instead of starving in the following winter, they might well have rallied. Without their horses, with few buffalo, unable to freely outmaneuver Mackenzie's scouting parties on the plains, and faced with terrible hardships in winter, they had little choice but to surrender. The Kiowas did so by February 1875, and the Comanches by June 1875, at Fort Sill. The final surrender of the Sioux to the north did not come about until after the virtual destruction of the northern buffalo herd and the failure of bison to cross in numbers into Canada from Montana after 1879.

A Change of Heart

Ironically, less than two years after the removal of the Comanches from the Palo Duro Canyon, in 1876, Colonel Charles Goodnight, who was to play a prominent role in the saving of bison from extinction, established his J.A. Ranch there. He found considerable numbers of bison in the canyon, most of which were slaughtered by hide hunters the following year.

That General Philip Sheridan eventually had second thoughts about wildlife extermination is one of the lasting ironies and the seed of North America's system of wildlife conservation. In 1866, however, he was still concerned about the scope of the effort to eliminate the buffalo. He tried to estimate the size of a buffalo herd extending some hundred miles across and of unknown length between Fort Supply and Fort Dodge, Kansas. He was greatly impressed by the sheer numbers of bison he saw on his travels. He speculated about their increased abundance in 1870 to 1871, suggesting that the poisoning with strychnine of wolves by wolfers and the lack of hunting by Indians too much engaged in warfare were the reasons.

Despite his tactic of exterminating buffalo to force the Native Americans to their knees, Sheridan took pleasure in bison. He organized several prestigious hunts for dignitaries and affluent acquaintances. And by 1882, he was much concerned about the mismanagement of Yellowstone National Park, in particular the killing of game by hide hunters, and he requested permission from the War Department to station army troops as protectors in the park, which was done in 1886. Two decades later, the army, as manager of Yellowstone National Park, played an important part in the bison's return from the brink of extinction.

The Canadian War on Bison

Throughout the 1800s, the buffalo was also destroyed on the Canadian plains. Canadian C. Gordon Hewitt recorded in *The Conservation of the Wild Life of Canada* published in 1921 that as early as 1857 the Plains Cree reported few bison ranging between the North and South Saskatchewan rivers and that the Cree tried to protect the remnants. However, as the northern bison moved from Montana and the Dakotas into Alberta and Saskatchewan, any depletion of the herds in the United States translated into fewer bison in Canada.

Métis Buffalo Hunters and the Fur Trade

The Métis people of the Canadian plains built a living on hunting buffalo for the Hudson's Bay Company in the 1800s. The first Métis communities emerged in the late 1600s around the Great Lakes and along the Red River Valley, the result of intermarriage between Native American women and French fur traders, trappers, voyageurs, and explorers, many of whom worked for the Hudson's Bay Company or its great rival, the Northwest Company. By the early 1800s, the Métis had proven themselves skillful buffalo hunters.

Within the Métis community, an intricate heirarchy was democratically created specifically for the annual or biannual buffalo hunt. Alexander Ross, sheriff of Assiniboia, Saskatchewan, recounted the Métis buffalo hunt for historian George Bryce's *The Remarkable History of the Hudson's Bay Company*, published in London in 1900. For a hunt in 1840, Ross observed a cavalcade of Métis some six miles (10 km) long traveling south to their hunting rendezvous at Pembina to organize the chase; included were 620 hunters, 650 women, 360 children, 542 dogs, 403 "buffalo runners" or hunting horses, 655 cart horses, 586 oxen, and 1,210 of the famed "Red River carts."

HERE, ON A level plain, the whole patriarchal camp squatted down like pilgrims on a journey to the Holy Land in ancient days, only not quite so devout, for neither scrip nor staff were consecrated for the occasion. Here the roll was called and general muster taken, when they numbered on this occasion 1630 souls; and here the rules and regulations for the journey were finally settled. The officials for the trip were named and installed into office, and all without the aid of writing materials. . . .

The first step was to hold a council for the nomination of chiefs or officers for conducting the expedition. Ten captains were named, the senior on this occasion being Jean Baptiste Wilkie, an English half-breed, brought up among the French, a man of good sound sense and long experience, and withal a fine, bold-looking, and discreet fellow, a second Nimrod in his way. Beside being captain, in common with the others, he was styled the great war chief or head of the camp, and on all public occasions he occupied the place of president. . . . Each captain had ten soldiers under his orders, in much the same way as policemen are subject to the magistrate.

The Métis council then "laid down the rules to be observed during the expedition": A flag would be hoisted every morning to raise the camp; no party was to run buffalo without permission; no buffalo were to be run on the Sabbath; and so on. As Ross recorded, "For the first trespass against these laws, the offender to have his saddle and bridle cut up. For the second offence the coat to be taken off the offender's back and to be cut up. For the third offence the offender to be flogged."

After traveling some 250 miles (400 km) over ten days, the Métis sighted an immense herd. Some 400 hunters mounted up and Captain Wilkie issued strict orders of strategy on how the hunt was to proceed. Then the hunt began:

IMAGINE 400 HORSEMEN entering at full speed a herd of some thousands of buffalo, all in rapid motion. Riders in clouds of dust and volumes of smoke which darken the air, crossing and recrossing each other in every direction; shots on the right, on the left, behind, before, here, there, two, three, a dozen at a time, everywhere in close succession, at the same moment. Horses stumbling, riders falling, dead and wounded animals tumbling here and there, one over the other; and this zigzag and bewildering *mêlée* continued for an hour or more together in wild confusion. . . .

The rider of a good horse seldom fires till within three or four yards of his object, and never misses. And, what is admirable in point of training, the moment the shot is fired his steed springs on one side to avoid stumbling over the animal, whereas an awkward and shy horse will not approach within ten or fifteen yards, consequently the rider has often to fire at random and not infrequently misses. Many of them, however, will fire at double that distance and make sure of every shot. The mouth is always full of balls; they load and fire at the gallop. . . .

On this occasion the surface was rocky, and full of badger holes. Twenty-three horses and riders were at one moment sprawling on the ground. One horse, gored by a bull, was killed on the spot, two men disabled by the fall. One rider broke his shoulder blade; another burst his gun and lost three of his fingers by the accident; and a third was struck on the knee by an exhausted ball. These accidents will not be thought over-numerous considering the result; for in the evening no less than 1375 buffalo tongues were brought into camp.

After two months of hunting, the Métis returned to settle accounts with the Hudson's Bay Company:

OUR ESTIMATE IS nine hundred pounds weight of buffalo meat per cart, a thousand being considered the full load, which gives one million and eighty-nine thousand pounds in all, or something more than two hundred pounds weight for each individual, old and young, in the settlement. . . . During the years 1839, 1840, and 1841, the [Hudson's Bay] Company expended five thousand pounds on the purchase of plain provisions, of which the hunters got last year the sum of twelve hundred pounds, being rather more money than all the agricultural class obtained for their produce in the same year.

Prairie of bone
Bleached by the sun, buffalo skulls and skeleton cover the ground near Lloydminster, Alberta. Some travelers reported that the prairies were so white with bones that they looked as if they were covered by snow. (Courtesy of the Saskatchewan Archives Board)

Each [Métis] hunter then filled his mouth with balls which he drops into the gun without wadding; by this means loading much quicker, and whilst his horse is at full speed. We now put our horses to the full gallop, and in twenty minutes were in their midst. There could not have been less than four or five thousand in our immediate vicinity, all bulls, not a single cow amongst them. The scene now became one of intense excitement: the huge bulls thundering over the plains in headlong confusion, whilst the fearless hunters rode recklessly in their midst, keeping up an incessant fire at but a few yards distance from their victims. Upon the fall of each buffalo the successful hunter merely threw some article of his apparel—often carried by him solely for that purpose—to denote his own prey, and then rushed on to another. These marks are scarcely ever disputed, but should a doubt arise as to the ownership, the carcase is equally divided between the claimants. The chase continued only about one hour, and extended over an area of from five to six square miles, over which might be seen the dead and dying buffaloes, to the number of five hundred.
—*Paul Kane,* Wanderings of an Artist among the Indians of North America, *1859*

The Canadian government did not declare war on the bison as the American government had done. Yet although it was not overt policy in Ottawa to destroy the bison, it is nevertheless likely that the presence of the bison was considered a nuisance. Just as in the United States, the bison herds encouraged independence in western Indian tribes and helped maintain the half-breed Métis, who ultimately rebelled against Ottawa in the Selkirk Incident, The Courthouse Rebellion, and the two Riel Rebellions.

Buffalo were extirpated from the Canadian plains just as effectively as in the United States without "benefit" of a military policy aimed at the destruction of native warriors. The Canadian government sought to assimilate Native People and settle them on reserves. The bison was decimated in Canada more for economic than political goals.

The grand old fur-trading firms such as the Hudson's Bay Company and the Northwest Company that had helped establish Canada saw the vast herds of buffalo as a commodity to be harvested. Bison were severely exploited by Métis and Native People servicing the fur trade, who—reluctantly—made bison skins objects of trade. Robes were the important trade items, and bison robes were accepted in order to keep the Native People in Canada from going south and trading with the Americans. Hunting for robes by Native People and Métis grew into a dependence on trade goods, while market forces created conditions for increased bison killing. As Plains Cree Edward Ahenakew grieved in the 1970s, "For twelve wolf-skins or three good buffalo-hides we got one blanket in trade. Chiefs who were chosen by the Hudson's Bay Company were given more than that, and their men brought them their furs to trade. Traders came to our encampments too, and it was always buffalo hides and pemmican they wanted. Hides. Hides. Shoot. Shoot. See who can shoot most. A curse upon man's greed and on the Crees for that inordinate slaughter."

With the northern herd collapsing in the United States, one expects its peripheral range to be empty of bison earlier than the center, which is more or less what happened as the bison were essentially gone from Alberta by April 1879. In 1883, a group of British sportsmen encountered a small herd of bison north of Calgary and killed fourteen of them. In 1884, the rumor that seven bison had been spotted in the Cy-

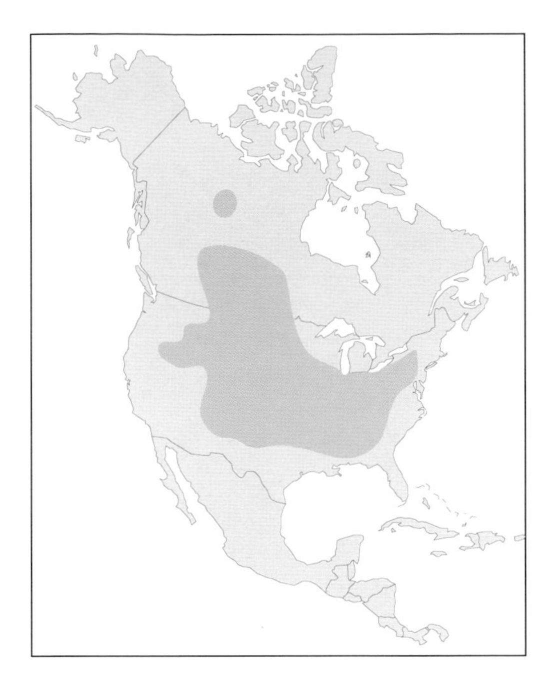

Range of the Buffalo at the dawn of the 1800s

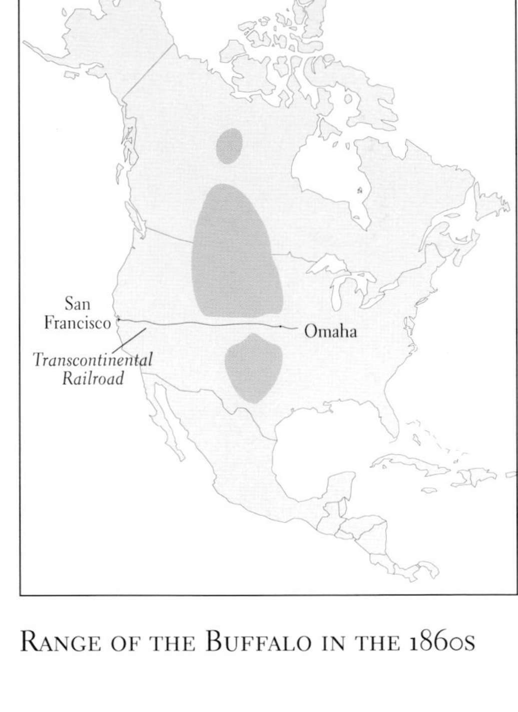

Range of the Buffalo in the 1860s

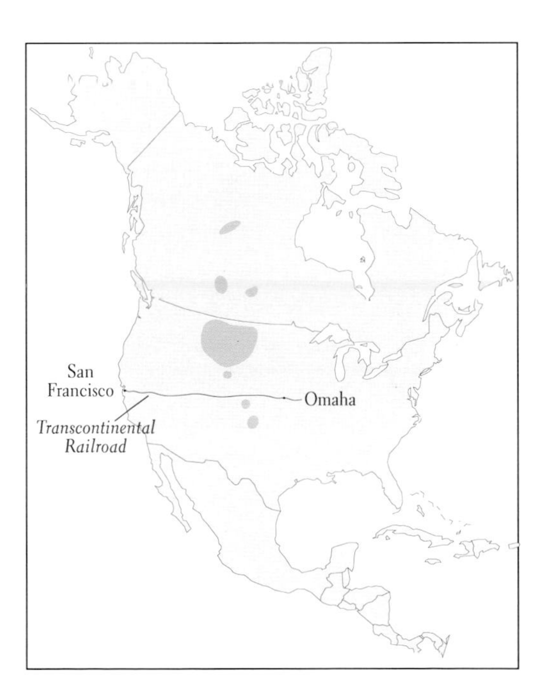

Range of the Buffalo in the 1880s

Killing the Last Buffalo in Montana

Nannie T. Alderson moved west in 1882 with her husband, Walt, to ranch in southeastern Montana. She wrote of the killing of what she believed was the last buffalo in Montana in her memoir, *A Bride Goes West*, published in 1942.

THE SUMMER AFTER I came out Mr. Alderson killed the last buffalo ever seen in our part of Montana. A man staying with us was out fishing when he saw this lonesome old bull wandering over the hills and gullies above our house—the first live buffalo seen in many months. He came home and reported it, saying: "Walt, why don't you go get him?" And next morning Mr. Alderson did go get him.

That afternoon he suggested that we take the spring wagon and go up to where the old bull had fallen. There he lay in the green brush at the bottom of a draw—the last of many millions—with the bushes propping him up so that he looked quite lifelike. I had brought my scissors, and I snipped a sackful of the coarse, curly hair from his mane to stuff a pillow with.

Land, land, rich meadow-land right up to where it met the sky in the blue distance. They stopped to look at the bleached skeleton of some huge animal; now what might that be? A buffalo, Erik answered; and went on to tell them how great herds of these stateliest animals of the prairie had once been there, until European sportsmen had come with their rifles, shooting, killing, and butchering them, without rhyme or reason. So the buffalo had been exterminated; and this was the skeleton of one of them.

—*Johan Bojer,* The Emigrants, *1925*

press Hills prompted a trainload of hunters to embark on the Canadian Pacific and disembark at Maple Creek. They did not succeed in finding their quarry.

The End of an Era

Some Europeans, sensitive to the fate of the land, warned of the buffalo's impending doom in the mid-1800s. Painter George Catlin wrote as early as 1842, "It seems hard and cruel, (does it not?) that we civilized people with all the luxuries and comforts of the world about us, should be drawing from the backs of these useful animals the skins for our luxury, leaving their carcasses to be devoured by the wolves—that we should draw from that country, some 150 or 200,000 of their robes annually, the greater part of which are taken from animals that are killed expressly for the robe, at a season when the meat is not cured and preserved, and for each of which skins the Indian has received but a pint of whiskey!" And naturalist John James Audubon stated in his *Missouri River Journals* published in 1843, "Daily we see so many [Buffalo] that we hardly notice them more than the cattle in our pastures about our homes. But this cannot last; even now there is a perceptible difference in the size of the herds, and before many years the Buffalo, like the Great Auk, will have disappeared; surely this should not be permitted."

By the turn of the century, bison were almost extinct. As Vice-Admiral Lindesay Brine wrote in his journal, *Travels Amongst American Indians, Their Ancient Earthworks and Temples* published in 1894, "The explorers who passed through these waste lands in the beginning of the nineteenth century, reported that the surface of the country, especially near the river Platte, was often blackened by immense herds of bisons. Fifty years later when I went over the same ground no buffaloes were to be seen there, and they no longer frequented that part of Nebraska."

A tiny herd survived in Yellowstone National Park, another in the Palo Duro Canyon of Texas, while in Canada there were three hundred to five hundred northern "wood bison" in northern Alberta and the Northwest Territories. The passenger pigeon had grown scarce and was about to disappear forever, as was the Eskimo curlew, a bird once unbelievably abundant, just as the bison had been. In the western states, stockmen had put an end to grizzly bears and wolves, a policy that was extended to national parks in order to save elk, deer, and wild sheep. Market hunting was still in force on waterfowl, song birds, and shore birds.

The near-extermination of the bison brought about a sobering realization that Nature had limits. Before and during the

First World War there was an examination of resource conservation in North America. And while this continental soul-searching about how wildlife was to be conserved and how the subsequent recommendations were to be implemented as policies and laws was overshadowed by the enormity of a terrible war, it had tangible consequences. A phoenix rose from the ashes of North America's destroyed wildlife—a new and effective system of wildlife conservation. It became the greatest environmental success story of the twentieth century, highly relevant to today's discussions about sustainable ecological development, global wildlife conservation, and the future of bison.

We, of those days, never could believe the buffalo would ever be killed off, for there were thousands and thousands.
—Métis Victoria Callihoo, "Our Buffalo Hunts," The Best from Alberta History

LONE SENTINEL
A buffalo skull rests in state on the prairie. (Photo © Layne Kennedy)

▲▲▲ Chapter 4 ▲▲▲

The Rise of the Phoenix

A cold wind blew across the prairie when the last buffalo fell . . .
a death-wind for my people.
—Hunkpapa Sioux Chief Sitting Bull

By the turn of the century, the war against the buffalo and the Native North Americans was over. While the Indians may have won the war, they lost the peace. And the war to exterminate the buffalo had been no contest: By 1889, rancher and conservationist Charles Jesse "Buffalo" Jones counted just 150 bison in all of the United States excluding the national parks. Jones wrote in his autobiography, *Buffalo Jones' Forty Years of Adventure* published in 1899, "A few years ago,—scarcely a quarter of a century,—millions upon millions of American bison roamed over the vast plains of the intracontinental region of North America. Now, they are so reduced in number that absolutely the last lingering spark of vitality is smoldering on the brink of extinction."

I sang to the spirits. Then my body became dead again, and my spirit saw many things. In my vision I saw these white men, like the countless buffalo, swarm across the land. I saw them build their houses by the rivers and the springs. I saw them taking our forests and killing our game, until the red men, women, and children cried for food. I heard children wail, I saw warriors and mothers sick with famine and disease. Then woe, woe! I saw all the nations of our land cry out, reaching their hands to the spirit people. And the cry brought no answer!

—*He Who Was Dead and Lives Again, quoted in* Indian Days of the Long Ago, *Edward S. Curtis, 1914*

ALONE ON THE HIGH PLAINS
Pages 100–101, main photo: *Two buffalo stand silhouetted on a spread of plains in Yellowstone National Park. (Photo © Tom Murphy)*

COMANCHE COW-BUFFALO EFFIGY
Page 101, inset: *This image was painted on a buffalo shoulder-blade bone, and was found on the plains in Comanche country of Texas in the mid-1800s. The effigy appears to be half buffalo, half cow, perhaps symbolizing the strife for the buffalo between Indians and the European settlers.*

With the buffalo no longer viewed by the American and Canadian governments as a strategic food supply to Native North Americans, a new—almost nostalgic—mood toward buffalo arose. As U.S. President Theodore Roosevelt, an active hunter as well as a conservationist, said in 1905, "The most characteristic animal of the western plains was the great shaggy-maned wild ox, the bison, commonly known as buffalo. Small fragments of herds exist in a domesticated state, here and there, a few of them in the Yellowstone Park. Such a herd as that on the Flathead reservation should not be allowed to go out of existence. Either on some reservation or on some forest reserve like the Wichita reserve or some refuge, provision should be made for the preservation of such a herd."

After the turn of the century, efforts to restore wildlife in the United States and Canada first bloomed. The movement was fostered by two befriended heads of state, America's Roosevelt and Canadian Prime Minister Sir Wilfrid Laurier. The task was executed by their able lieutenants, Gifford Pinchot in the United States and Clifford Sifton in Canada.

They were aided in turn by the popularizers of wildlife's plight, foremost among whom were American William T. Hornaday and Canadian C. Gordon Hewitt. While he was not a good historian, Hornaday was a brave, resourceful spokesperson on behalf of wildlife and wrote several books that included conservation pleas. Hewitt was the architect of the 1916 U.S.–Canadian migratory bird treaty and wrote the first Canadian call to arms, *The Conservation of the Wild Life of Canada*. He never saw it in print as he fell victim to the influenza epidemic that swept much of Canada in 1919.

Beginning in 1908 in the United States and 1911 in Canada, national commissions on conservation led to continental wildlife treaties, policies, and laws that reversed wildlife's decline, returned species from the edge of extinction, and allowed the numbers of wildlife to rise to at least modest abundance. The number of wild large mammals in the United States and Canada rose to more than thirty million by the late 1970s, which is believed to be more than three times the population in 1958.

This conservation system also saved some large predators from extinction, fostered the growth of an extensive system of protected areas and thus of biodiversity, taxed the public—in particular taxing users of wildlife on behalf of wildlife—engendered many organizations that spoke up for conservation, and led to the development of wildlife management as a new science-based profession. North America's system of wildlife conservation is thus a rare example of successful ecologically sustainable development.

Saving the Buffalo Herds

Bison were saved initially by six individuals who either saw business opportunities in the existence of bison or simply wanted to save a vanishing species. Beginning in the 1870s, these six men captured the bison from which virtually all plains bison have descended: James McKay, Charles Alloway, Charles Goodnight, Walking Coyote, Frederic Dupree, and Charles "Buffalo" Jones. When these private bison herds grew and generated problems, however, the private owners tried to unburden themselves by placing the bison in public

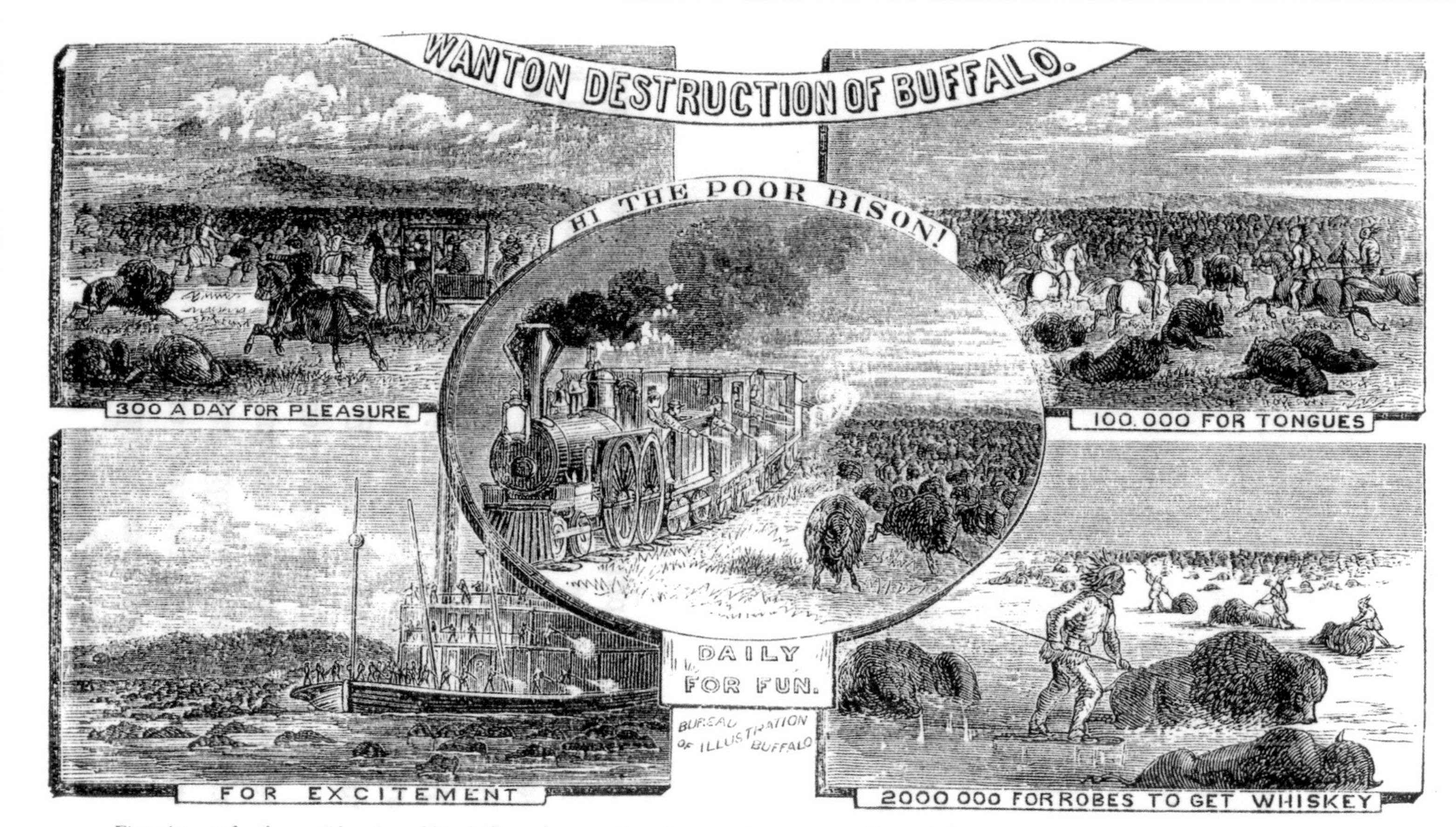

"WANTON DESTRUCTION OF BUFFALO"
A satirical but all too true cartoon bemoaning the coming extirpation of the bison. Drawn by Henry Worrall, it was printed in W. E. Webb's Buffalo Land *tourist chronicle of 1872.*

hands. The U.S. and Canadian governments came late to the rescue of bison and were at first rather ineffectual, despite urgency voiced by the public.

As a species, all bison living today come from a narrow genetic base. After the destruction of the last large herds at the end of the nineteenth century, there were few remnants of free-roaming plains bison, scattered in various areas. Despite efforts to save them, by 1902 the free-roaming buffalo had all died out except for a small herd of twenty-three bison left in Yellowstone National Park; there was an additional small herd of bison in the Palo Duro Canyon of Texas that has survived to this day. The U.S. Army's valiant attempt at protecting Yellowstone's wildlife notwithstanding, those twenty-three animals were all that escaped the determined efforts of poachers killing for profit. All plains bison other than the Yellowstone herd originated from eighty-eight bison, mainly calves, captured between 1873 and 1889.

"Buffalo" Jones captured fifty-six calves in northern Texas. To these he added ten adult bison purchased from individuals in Nebraska and Kansas. "Sam"

The Ghost Dance

I shall cut off his feet, I shall cut off his feet
I shall cut off his head, I shall cut off his head
He gets up again, he gets up again
—Kiowa ghost dance song for the resurrection of the buffalo

By the 1880s, the war to exterminate the buffalo was having its designed effect in forcing Native Americans to resettle on the U.S. government's designated reservations. Many chose reservation life with the promises of food and supplies as well as buffalo hunting rights to specified lands "so long as the buffalo may range thereon in such numbers as to justify the chase," as stated in article 11 of the 1868 Treaty establishing the Great Sioux reservation. The days of the buffalo, however, were fast coming to an end.

From out of this war of genocide on the Native Americans came a prophet in the form of a Paiute holy man named Wovoka. He preached a message of a coming millennium that would restore the Indians' world to a time before the white settlers arrived and buffalo were plentiful.

Wovoka insisted that all Native Americans practice the Ghost Dance. The sacred dance and trance that it induced would "roll up the world" and then unroll it anew. The dance would send away all the white people, rejuvenate the land, bring back ancestors and buffalo, and all the tribes would live in abundance and peace. As Wovoka intoned, "All Indians must dance, everywhere, keep on dancing. Pretty soon in next spring Great Spirit come. He bring back all game of every kind. The game be thick everywhere. All dead Indians come back and live again. They all be strong just like young men, be young again."

Other tribes sent emissaries to learn of Wovoka's teachings, including Lakota Chief Kicking Bear, who told his people of his conversation to the Ghost Dance: "[The Great Spirit] will cover the earth with new soil to a depth of five times the height of a man, and under this new soil will be buried all the whites, and all the holes and rotten places will be filled up. The new lands will be covered with sweet-grass and running water and trees, and herds of buffalo and ponies will stray over it, that my red children may eat and drink, hunt and rejoice."

The Ghost Dance was an apocalyptic religion in an apocalyptic time. As James Welch described it in *Killing Custer*, "The Ghost Dance was a frenzied affair, with much whirling and shrieking and praying, until people would drop from exhaustion and convulse and have visions."

Naturally, the Ghost Dance invoked fear in the Indian agents, government, and the army. Major James McLaughlin, the U.S. Indian Agent at Standing Rock Agency, sent a report on the dancing to T. J. Morgan, U.S. Commissioner of Indian Affairs in Washington, D.C., on October 17, 1890. The message bore more than a slight hint of fear:

I DO FEEL IT my duty to report the present "craze" and nature of the excitement existing among the "Sitting Bull" faction of Indians over the expected "Indian Millennium," the annihilation of the white man, and supremacy of the Indian, which is looked for in the near future and promised by the Indian "Medicine Men" as not later than next spring, when the new grass begins to appear, and is known among the Sioux as the "return of the Ghosts."

They are promised by some members of the Sioux tribe, who have lately developed into "medicine Men," that the Great Spirit has promised them that their punishment by the dominant race has been sufficient and that their numbers having now become so decimated will be reinforced by all Indians who are dead; that the dead are all returning to re-inhabit this earth which belongs to the Indians; that they are driving back with them as they return, immense herds of buffalo and elegant wild horses to have for the catching; that the Great Spirit promises that the white man will be unable to make gunpowder in future and all attempts at such will be a failure and that the gunpowder now on hand will be useless as against Indians, as it will not throw a bullet with sufficient force to pass through the skin of an Indian; that the Great Spirit has deserted the Indians for a long period but is now with them and against the whites, and will cover the earth over with thirty feet of additional soil, well sodded and timbered, under which the whites will all be smothered, and any whites who may escape this great phenomena will become small fishes in the rivers of the country, but in order to bring about this happy results the Indians must do their part and become believers and thoroughly organized.

It would seem impossible that any person, no matter how ignorant, could be brought to believe such absurd nonsense, but as a matter of fact a great many Indians of this Agency actually believe it. . . .

On November 25, 1890, McLaughlin reported again, still attempting to laugh at the Ghost Dance: "It is wonderful to see how zealous the ordinary Indians are in their faith of this false Christ, their credulity and inherent superstition making them an easy prey to the more wily prophets and cunning impostors of Medicine Men, while the Chief Priests seem to succeed in deceiving themselves as well as each other in their misleading nonsense and extending the foolish craze, and while there are but few Indians brave enough to express themselves as not believing in the new doctrine."

Part of the reason for the agents' concern was that Wovoka promised that if the dancers wore a sacred Ghost shirt, it would protect them from the bullets of the whites. This inspired a fearless resistance in the dancers, and the agents foresaw the bloodshed that would come in the following years.

The government's response was to outlaw the Ghost Dance and crush the resistance anywhere and everywhere. The finale came on December 29, 1890, when more than two hundred Minneconjou and Hunkpapa Sioux were massacred by the U.S. Seventh Cavalry at Wounded Knee in the Dakota Territory. The Ghost shirts were not bulletproof.

Arapaho Ghost Dance shirt
Made circa 1885 at the height of the Ghost Dance movement, this shirt was believed to protect its wearer from the bullets of the white men. This shirt was later purchased from a follower by a European settler in 1916. (Courtesy of the Logan Museum of Anthropology, Beloit College: The Albert Green Heath Collection. Photo © Michael Simon)

"CONQUERED AT LAST"
Or so stated the original note handwritten on this photograph of Charles J. "Buffalo" Jones driving a wagon pulled by a buffalo team. This image is rather ironic as Jones was in fact one of six people responsible for saving the bison from extinction. At the turn of the century, bison were seen by entrepreneurs as potential money makers for their owners. Bison were saved less for cultural than for business reasons and played a role in the entertainment world as well, most prominently in Buffalo Bill's Wild West Show. Buffalo Jones, meanwhile, used this team to work his Kansas ranch, at times hitching the bison to plow fields in springtime. (Courtesy of the Kansas State Historical Society)

These broad, grassy plains are not yet entirely destitute of their former inhabitants; flocks of antelope still feed on the rich, nutritious grasses; but the buffalo, which once roamed here by the thousands, have disappeared forever. No trace of them is now left but the old trails, which pass across the country in every direction, and the bleached skulls which are scattered here and there over the ground. These traces are fast passing away. The skulls are decaying rapidly, and this once peculiar feature of the landscape in the West will be lost. Two years ago I collected a large quantity of these bleached skulls and distributed them to several of our museums, in order to insure their preservation.
—*W. E. Webb,* Buffalo Land, *1872*

Walking Coyote, a member of the Pend d'Oreille tribe, captured a number of calves in northern Montana or southern Alberta. Of these, four survived to start the famous Pablo-Allard herd. In Saskatchewan, the Alloway brothers captured five calves and Samuel Bedson of Stoney Plains, Manitoba, captured three. Five calves and two adult bison formed the nucleus of Charles Goodnight's herd in Texas. The origin of Frederic Dupree's herd was five calves captured along the Yellowstone River. Dupree's five were the only bison from captured stock that did not contribute to the genetics of the plains bison assembled by the Canadian government by 1914 in Alberta in the now-closed Buffalo National Park near Wainwright and Elk Island National Park near Edmonton. A few additional bison held in zoos may also have contributed genetically to today's plains bison.

The northern bison survived in slightly larger numbers than the plains bison. In the 1890s, the herd of northern bison in what is now Wood Buffalo National Park, Alberta, may have shrunk to 300 to 500 animals; it is even possible that as few as 250 survived.

Allowing for the fact that we do not know how many of the captured calves grew up to reproduce, all North American bison alive today are likely descended from fewer than three hundred individuals, including northern bison: the eighty-eight captured bison, the twenty-three in Yellowstone, and a few in zoos. Moreover, there must have been a loss of genetic information due to low numbers in founder herds, genetic drift, and above all, by the displacement from breeding by dominant bulls of a large number of lower-ranking bulls—that is, only a few of the male bison rescued from oblivion succeeded in passing their genes on to future generations.

The various herds in private hands were soon mixed, and some genetic pollution took place when cattalo (hybrids of cattle and bison) were mixed with bison. Walking Coyote's four calves were brought to the Flathead Reservation in Montana, where the bison multiplied. In 1883, twelve of these bison were bought by M. Pablo and C. A. Allard. In 1893, twenty-six bison from the herd of Charles Jones were added to the Pablo-Allard, while an additional eighteen cattalo were isolated on Wild Horse Island in Flathead Lake. Jones, in

▲▲▲ Native North American Legends ▲▲▲

The Passing of the Buffalo

The buffalo was believed to have come from a cave or hole in the ground. Native American stories tell of the last buffalo to leave the earth returning underground.

This Kiowa tale of the passing of the buffalo is similar to stories recounted in varying forms by storytellers of many tribes:

In the beginning, the buffalo came from the earth, and in the end, the buffalo went back into the earth.

The people were at war with the white man's army, who were chasing them across what was once their land. The people were hungry and had no food; they were afraid of the army, yet had to search for food and water.

One day, a Kiowa woman awoke early and went from her camp in the mountains down to a spring to get water. The sun was not yet up and the valley was filled with mist. As the women knelt down to get water, she saw something mysterious in the mist.

Out of the mist came an old buffalo cow leading a herd of wounded and tired buffalo and a few small calves. She had not seen a buffalo for a long time. This was the last herd of buffalo to still survive.

As she watched, the old buffalo cow led the last herd through the mist and toward the mountain. Then the mountain opened up before them, and inside of the mountain the earth was fresh and young. The sun shone brightly and the water was clear. The earth was green and the sky blue. Into this beautiful land walked the last herd of buffalo and the mountain closed.

The buffalo were gone.

Reader! listen to the following calculations, and forget them not. The buffaloes (the quadrupeds from whose backs your beautiful robes were taken, and whose myriads were once spread over the whole country, from the Rocky Mountains to the Atlantic Ocean) have recently fled before the appalling appearance of civilized man. . . . It is a melancholy contemplation for one who has travelled as I have through these realms, and seen this noble animal in all its pride and glory, to contemplate it so rapidly wasting from the world, drawing the irresistible conclusion too, which one must do, that its species is soon to be extinguished, and with it the peace and happiness (if not the actual existence) of the tribes of Indians who are joint tenants with them, in the occupancy of these vast and idle plains.
—*George Catlin,* Letters and Notes on the Manners, Customs, and Condition of the North American Indians, *1842*

GRAZING HERD
A bison herd grazes on prairie grasses on a misty morning in Yellowstone National Park. Only in recent years with the reintroduction of gray wolves is the Yellowstone ecosystem close to restoration. The wolf reintroduction will also make Yellowstone buffalo the only American herd that, by re-adapting to wolf predation, would reverse the effects of inadvertent domestication. (Photo © Alan and Sandy Carey)

Prairies of Bone

Following in the footsteps of the buffalo hunters came the bone pickers. Descriptions abound of the great plains reeking with the stench of putrefying buffalo carcasses that later decayed into prairies of bones. Several entrepreneurs saw these bones as dollar signs.

Just as Native North Americans had subsisted on the many parts of the buffalo, the Europeans now created dramatically new uses for the bison. Buffalo hide found a ready market due to its plasticity and was tanned for many uses, including as belts to drive factory machinery in the industrial East. Buffalo tongues were butchered, salted, and sold as a delicacy. Robes—especially those of white buffalo—were in high demand to tailor into fashionable coats. Even the bison's coarse hair and beard was used for upholstery stuffing. The bone pickers gave the buffalo one final hurrah of sorts: The bones, hooves, and horns were shipped back east, ground, and used in refining sugar and for fertilizer.

Traveling west on the Canadian Pacific in 1888, Julian Ralph wrote of the bone-filled plains and the big business that sprouted up to collect and sell the buffalo's remains:

At the outset we saw a few bison bones dotting the grass in white specks here and there, and soon we met great trains, each of many box cars, laden with nothing but these weather-whitened relics. Presently, we came to stations where, beside the tracks, mounds of these bones were heaped up and rude men were swelling the heaps with wagon loads gathered far from the railroads, for a great business had grown up in collecting these trophies.

The size of the business was indeed gigantic—at least while supplies lasted. In her book *The Buffalo Hunters*, historian Mari Sandoz provided the following example of but one company's activity: "One bone-buying firm estimated that over the seven years, 1884–1891 they bought the bones of approximately five million, nine hundred and fifty thousand buffalo skeletons, and there were many firms in the business."

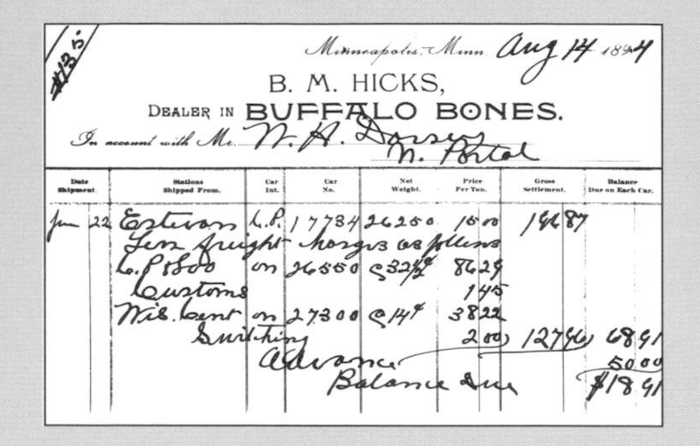

#135

Minneapolis, Minn Aug 14 1894

B. M. HICKS,

DEALER IN BUFFALO BONES.

In account with Mr. N. A. Dorsey N. Portal

Date Shipment	Stations Shipped From.	Car Int.	Car No.	Net Weight.	Price Per Ton.	Gross Settlement.	Balance Due on Each Car.
Jun 22	Estevan	L.P.	17734	26250	15 00	196 87	
	Less freight charges as follows						
	L.P. 8800 on 26550 @ 32½¢				86 29		
	Customs				1 45		
	Wis. Cent on 27300 @ 14¢				38 22		
	Switching				2 00	127 96	68 91
	Advance						50 00
	Balance Due						$18 91

"B. M. Hicks, Dealer in Buffalo Bones"

A receipt for an August 1894 shipment of buffalo bones that filled three railroad cars. (Courtesy of the Saskatchewan Archives Board)

Métis bone collectors

Métis buffalo-bone collectors stand amid mounds of bones bleached by the Canadian prairie sun. The bones were collected on the prairies in Red River carts such as the one pictured here. They were then loaded onto railroad cars and transported to factories in the east to be ground and used in refining sugar or for fertilizer. (Courtesy of the Saskatchewan Archives Board)

The bone business made money all along its route, from settlers who supported themselves collecting bones to the freighters who carried them. In its early days, Regina, Saskatchewan, served as a railhead where bones were deposited for freighting east. Before being tagged with its current, more refined name, Regina was known as Pile o' Bones for its industry.

In the heyday of the buffalo hunters, the railroads shipped massive quantities of hides and meat back east; now they filled boxcars with bones. Explorer Colonel Richard Dodge recorded that in the boom year of 1873, the railroads carried a total of 754,329 hides, 4,852,800 pounds (2,183,760 kg) of meat, and 8,229,300 pounds (3,703,185 kg) of bones. In 1874, they hauled a total of 20 million pounds (9,000,000 kg) of bones to refineries.

Perhaps more telling as to the fate of the buffalo was how quickly the business died. The St. Paul & Chicago Rail Road freighted east 35,000 to 40,000 hides and 10,000 robes in 1882. In 1885, they shipped next to none.

CHARGING BUFFALO HERD
A herd of bison on the run in Yellowstone National Park. Early North American bison were by far faster than their modern siblings. Close studies of their respective skeletons reveal that early bison were geared for speed as they faced a rich array of large, fast-running predators. (Photo © Layne Kennedy)

turn, had bought in 1889 some fifty-eight Saskatchewan bison and eight cattalo from Samuel Bedson. Bedson's bison comprised the McKay-Alloway herd that originated from five calves captured in Saskatchewan in 1873 to 1874 plus the additional three calves captured by Bedson in Saskatchewan. Thus, the Pablo-Allard herd contained bison captured originally in Montana or Alberta, Saskatchewan, Texas, and probably individuals from Kansas and Nebraska. Those bison in Bedson's herd that did not go to the Pablo-Allard herd went to Sir Donald A. Smith, who donated thirteen of them to Banff National Park. Those thirteen were joined by three Texas bison from Charles Goodnight's herd, brought to Banff in 1887.

The U.S. Army responded to the decline in the Yellowstone herd by purchasing fourteen bison cows from the Pablo-Allard herd in Montana and three bulls

WATERING HOLE
Buffalo watering in the Little Missouri River running through Theodore Roosevelt National Park in North Dakota. Water is a dangerous place for bison as wolves can easily prey on them here; these "snow dogs" with their enlarged paws can readily overtake swimming buffalo and dismember them in the water. In winter, frozen but snow-covered lakes are sought out by bison trying to outrun wolves. Then the lakes are dangerous only when the ice is snow-free and slick. (Photo © Michael H. Francis)

In my book a pioneer is a man who turned all the grass upside down, strung bob-wire over the dust that was left, poisoned the water and cut down the trees, killed the Indian who owned the land, and called it progress. If I had my way, the land here would be like God made it, and none of you sons of bitches would be here at all.
—Charles M. Russell, Montana cowboy painter, speaking to Great Falls, Montana, civic boosters, 1920s

from the Goodnight herd in Texas. The army placed the bison into an enclosure along with some calves caught from the wild Yellowstone herd. This led to a buffalo ranch in the park that was run along military lines, with hay grown on irrigated meadows and some bulls being castrated and branded like cattle. A few bulls were released into the wild. By 1907, there were sixty-one bison in captivity in Yellowstone; by 1916, there were seventy-two wild bison, while the captive herd numbered 273. The Yellowstone bison had been saved. Although domestication was only short-term, it generated a serious problem—the captive bison contracted bovine brucellosis, which they passed on to wild elk in the park. The transmission of the disease set the stage for future challenges to the bison from the agricultural industry.

Between June 1, 1907, and June 6, 1912, M. Pablo delivered to Canadian authorities 716 bison, of which 631 went to Buffalo National Park and the remaining 85 went to Elk Island National Park. On October 1909, 77 bison were added to the herd in Buffalo National Park from Banff, and 10 more were delivered on March 31, 1914. In 1910 and 1911, 30 more bison were delivered to Buffalo National Park from the Conrad herd near Kalispell, Montana; these bison originated from the Allard estate. Therefore, the bison assembled in Buffalo National Park by 1914 were a mixture of southern and northern plains bison.

Some 6,673 plains bison—4,826 yearlings, 1,515 two-year-olds, and 332 three-year-olds, predominantly females—were shipped to Wood Buffalo National Park from Buffalo National Park beginning on June 25, 1925, over the protests of zoologists. Many of the bison did not survive the relocation. Tuberculosis surfaced in Buffalo National Park as early as 1919, and the bison transferred in 1925 were carriers of bovine tuberculosis and brucellosis. Since tuberculosis lesions appeared primarily in adult bison, it had been thought that shipping young bison would not transfer the disease. No such luck. Subsequently, the transferred bison bred with native wood bison and probably infected them with the diseases, although tuberculosis was not identified in Wood Buffalo National Park until 1937 and brucellosis not until 1956. While the mixing of plains and wood bison genetically may have been a negligible tragedy, the infection of bison in Wood Buffalo National Park with livestock diseases was not.

The Genetic Bottleneck

All bison in North America, except the small Palo Duro Canyon herd in Texas, are a mixture of bison from across the continent—plus an occasional admixture of domestic cattle. Bison, in the process of being saved, have gone through severe genetic bottlenecks, most of which were imposed by the management process.

All herds were subject to genetic distortions during establishment. These include differences based on the *founder effect* (reduction of genetic diversity due to the small sample of bison to found new herds), *genetic drift* (random fixation of alleles, or genes, in small populations), the *maternal effect* (bison captured from the same herd have a high probability of being related by maternal descent and thus have reduced genetic diversity), and the *male dominance effect* (disproportionate genetic contribution of the most dominant

Searching for water
A lone buffalo drinks from a rare source of open water in the midst of winter in Yellowstone National Park. In the summer, water fulfills the bison's metabolic water demand; in the winter, buffalo often are forced to rely on snow. (Photo © Tom Murphy)

COATED IN SNOW

Snow-covered buffalo winter in Yellowstone National Park. Snow is not only a barrier to finding food, it also increases the cost of movements for wintering bison. But snow also protects vegetation, conserving its nutritive value while allowing some grasses to grow under its protection. When the ground is blanketed by snow, bison clear it from their forage with sweeping actions of their heads. Dry, powdery snow combined with cold temperatures allows them ready access to covered grasses. (Photo © Tom Murphy)

Bison cow and calf
A buffalo cow nuzzles her calf in Banff National Park, Alberta. (Photo © James P. Rowan)

founder bull in tiny founding populations).

For instance, a founding herd of "wood bison" was captured on the Nyarling River near Needle Lake, Northwest Territories, and turned loose in Elk Island National Park in the fall of 1965. The herd consisted of only four bulls and seventeen cows taken from a small and possibly relict population of as few as ninety-seven bison. The females almost certainly were related by maternal descent, and the bulls captured probably were related to the cows. Consequently, it was in all likelihood an inbred population. Subsequently, social competition among the four bulls in the founding herd ensured that only one bull bred virtually all the cows for four to six years, including, after three to four years, his own daughters. Then he would have been displaced by his sons. These, grown to larger size on the unoccupied, rich range, likely displaced their father, and bred their mothers, aunts, sisters, and cousins.

Small founder populations of bison such as these rapidly become inbred, reducing the value of the herd taxonomically, scientifically, and as a source of breeding stock. Letting small founder herds grow into large populations without counteracting maternal effect, genetic drift, and the male dominance effect is not good conservation management.

Only one of the bison herds surviving today lives in an environment with its historic complement of predators, on its original range, and under near-normal ecological conditions: the Wood Buffalo National Park herd. Even here this herd has had an adventuresome history of mismanagement. This includes the introduction of plains bison and livestock diseases; severe wolf control; failed measures at disease control with massive mortality due to herding; slaughter to supply surrounding communities with meat; and in recent years, massive habitat loss and drowning losses due to the construction of the W.A.C. Bennett Dam on the Peace River in British Columbia. Under severe predation by wolves, the herd declined from about

The Spotted Buffalo

There is power in a buffalo—spiritual, magic power—but there is no power in an Angus, in a Hereford.
—John (Fire) Lame Deer, *Lame Deer Seeker of Visions*, with Richard Erdoes, 1972

The buffalo were replaced by domesticated cattle and barbed-wire was strung up on fenceposts to divide the Great Plains into privately owned allotments. Called "spotted buffalo" by some, the domesticated cow was viewed with disdain by most Native North Americans. In his autobiography, Chief Buffalo Child Long Lance spoke of the end of the buffalo and the coming of the spotted buffalo:

I USED TO go to my room at night [in the mission school] and lie and think of the old days when there were buffalo and plenty of animals everywhere. . . . Then I would think of what my old grandfather used to tell me when I was a small child. He said that some day the white man would be everywhere on the plains. I did not believe him. He said that some day they would drive all of the animals away; they would put up fences everywhere, and the Indian would have to camp in one place all of the time. I did not believe him. But now I was beginning to realize that everything my grandfather said was coming true—and I wondered if he could see it.

In one of his several remembrances of things past, *My People the Sioux*, Luther Standing Bear recounted the first time he saw a cow—and his revulsion:

ONE DAY WE boys heard some of the men talking about going to the agency. They said the Government had sent some spotted buffalo for the Indians. This was the name the Indians gave to the cows, there being no word in the Sioux tongue for the white man's cattle. Our own wild buffalo had been disappearing very rapidly, as the white people had been killing them as fast as possible. We were happy to learn that we were to receive more meat, this being our main diet. We had heard about these spotted buffalo, but had never seen them.

So we got on our ponies and rode over to the agency with some of the men. What a terrible odor met us! It was awful! We had to hold our noses. Then I asked my father what was the matter around there, as the stench was more than I could stand. He told me it was the odor of the spotted buffalo. Then I asked him if we were going to be obliged to eat those terrible animals.

I have hunted buffalo in this country many times. I feel lonesome since the buffalo have been driven away. . . . My people used to hunt buffalo in this part of the country, and I could see trails of these large animals now worn deep by the storms of many years, and I cried in my heart.
—Chief Umapine, Cayuse tribe of the Umatillas, Oregon, 1904

SEARCHING FOR FOOD
The trail of a lone buffalo through the snow marks its passage as it searches for forage in the midst of winter in Yellowstone National Park. (Photo © Tom Murphy)

12,000 in 1934 to about 2,000 bison in 1994.

The controversy about the mixing of plains and wood bison in the Wood Buffalo herd is a threat to its future, as is the presence of tuberculosis and brucellosis due to Agriculture Canada's drive for a tuberculosis-free status for Canada's livestock. While this is the most severely tested bison herd by predators and natural factors, and thus the most valuable gene pool for the species *Bison bison*, it is not a secure herd. The bison here have no future as long as they are regarded by members of the regulatory agencies established to insure their welfare, let alone by Canadian agricultural bureaucracies, as "worthless diseased hybrids."

The next most important bison herd is in Yellowstone National Park and numbers some 3,500 individuals living in a secure 2.2-million-acre park along with much native flora and fauna. This area was marginal for bison, historically containing only small herds on meadows surrounded by forests. Grizzly bears still prey on these bison; wolves, missing for decades, were reintroduced in 1995. The herd is a mixture of northern, southern, and indigenous "mountain" bison. It is infected with bovine brucellosis, which has been passed on to elk in the park.

Now that the Yellowstone herd is expanding, it has been branded a threat to the cattle industry, even though the brucella organism is currently transmitted virtually only in mother's milk. Infected aborted fetuses and placentas that are potentially dangerous to cattle, but abortions in these bison have not been detected for a long time. More than one thousand bison have stepped outside the park and been killed, and the herd has been subject to litigation. It is fairly secure, but it would be more secure without brucellosis.

The third most important bison herd lives in the Mackenzie Bison Sanctuary north of Great Slave Lake in the Canadian Northwest Territories. This is a relatively recent herd based on a 1963 release of sixteen bison from the Nyarling River herd. It has grown to more than 2,000 and, like the Wood Buffalo herd, is exposed to wolf predation as well as natural factors. Unfortunately, it is highly inbred and lives not in a national park but merely on a territorial "sanctuary." This herd appears to be slated for meat production and subsistence and trophy hunting. If its genetic base could be diversified, if its existence as a free-roaming, unhunted herd could be assured, then this could become the most important herd for bison conservation as it is not infected with livestock diseases. There is a small but real chance that bison straying across Great Slave Lake may infect this herd with bovine tuberculosis and brucellosis. And recently this herd has experienced severe mortality from anthrax.

There are three recent Canadian herds of bison with natural predators and conditions. Two were established from the inbred Nyarling River "wood bison" held in Elk Island National Park, and one is descended from escaped plains bison that had been bought to create a commercial bison ranch. These are the Nahanni-Liard herd in the Northwest Territories and northern British Columbia, the Nissling River herd in Yukon, and the Pink Mountain herd in northern British Columbia.

The Nahanni herd was established in 1980 from twenty-eight founders, to which twelve more bison were added in 1989.

Plains Cree buffalo skull image
This dramatic bison skull was painted in the 1980s on a pair of leggings that were part of a Canadian Plains Cree woman's jingle-dance pow-wow costume.

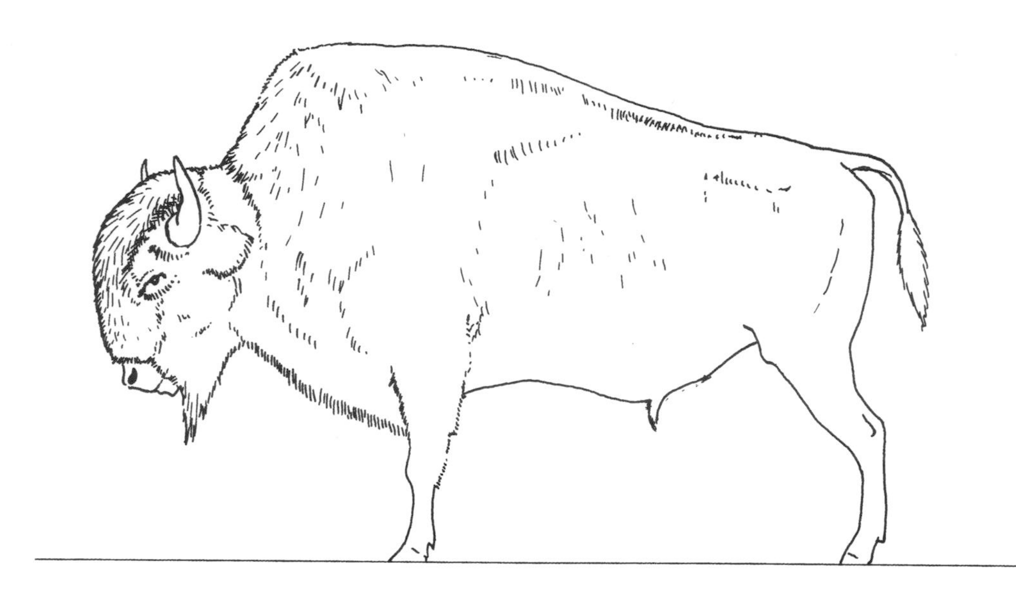

WOOD BISON, PHANTOM SUBSPECIES
The wood bison was named a subspecies Bison bison athabascae *late in the nineteenth century. Northern bison had been brought to Elk Island National Park in Alberta, where these large "wood bison" developed with a distinctly different hair coat from plains bison. Peter Karsten and I reported this in the scientific literature in 1977, and our description "codified" the appearance of "wood bison"; the National Museum of Canada confirmed the "subspecies." Wood Buffalo National Park bison, meanwhile, are indigenous northern bison with an admixture of plains bison introduced in 1925. A blue-ribbon Canadian government committee recommended slaughtering all these bison and replacing them with "pure" Elk Island stock as Wood Buffalo bison were deemed "worthless hybrids" as well as carriers of tuberculosis and brucellosis. In the meantime, I discovered that "wood bison" transformed miraculously into perfectly good "plains bison" if removed from Elk Island and held elsewhere in captivity or released to the wild. Wood bison were thus not a subspecies but an ecotype, a form reflecting environmental conditions due to confinement and a shortage of nutrients to finish growing their hair coats. Secondly, the National Museum used inappropriate methods to determine subspecific distinction. Wood bison are thus a phantom subspecies, which was later confirmed by genetic research. The hybrid argument did not hold, nor did much of what the blue-ribbon panel said, and due to public pressure, the Canadian government reversed its recommendation. The bison of Wood Buffalo National Park are alive and doing well today. (Drawing by Valerius Geist)*

This herd, which initially fragmented and dispersed, is growing slowly; in 1992 it numbered only some sixty bison. It may be in the path of the expanding Pink Mountain herd of plains bison. The bison are not in a national park or sanctuary, but they are likely to be secure—if they succeed in establishing themselves. Depending on their expansion, they are likely to be hunted.

The Nissling River herd was established in 1986 from thirty-four Nyarling River bison from Elk Island National Park. Ten calves from Nyarling River bison held in the wild animal park in Moose Jaw, Saskatchewan, whose parents originally came from Elk Island National Park, were added in 1989. Additional releases of Nyarling River bison from Elk Island National Park were expected to raise this herd to two hundred by 1994. This herd is well outside historic bison range, and while the Nissling River area in Pleistocene times must have been covered by extensive loess steppe and was excellent bison habitat, the current ecological conditions mitigate against anything but a small, relict-type bison population—provided it can survive at all. An earlier introduction of plains bison in the same general area failed, and bison introduced to Alaska to similar ecological conditions survive largely due to subsidies from agriculture. No population explosion of bison can be expected here.

The Pink Mountain herd in British Columbia originated from fifty-five Elk Island National Park plains bison that were sold into private ownership in 1971 but subsequently escaped. Because of its origin from plains bison, rather than inbred Nyarling River "wood" bison, this genetically superior herd is not in favor and it's been suggested that they be replaced with "real wood bison." With bison ranching going strong, we can expect additional feral mixed bison herds in northern Canada.

Nyarling River bison have been dispersed to eleven zoological gardens: six in Canada, two in the United States, and three in Germany. They also exist as captives on two ranches—Hanging Ice Ranch and Waterhen Wood Bison Ranches—and in Elk Island National Park. These bison are thus subject to inadvertent selection for domestication. The zoo herds are managed genetically by means of a stud book. These captive bison, now under private control, are a potential resource to fall back upon should there be accidental extinctions of other herds.

A small, wild herd of northern bison exists under natural conditions on public land outside Wood Buffalo National Park at Hook Lake. This herd is currently in need of genetic salvage and safeguard. It may otherwise be lost.

A large number of captive herds are found in the United States and Canada on public land in national parks and sanctuaries of various sizes. These herds are exposed to native climates and vegetation to varying degrees, but are not exposed to predators such as wolves and grizzly bears. They are largely, but not all, pure plains bison; some contain cattle genes. Their value to conservation is proportional to the herd size and inversely related to the duration of their captivity. Large herds on large tracts of land and little hindered by fences are more likely to remain close to the native genotype of bison, while small herds closely managed and in contact with humans are likely to be more altered by domestication and inbreeding. A small herd of pure Texas bison that survives in the Palo Duro Canyon is genetically valuable and potentially a boon to plains bison conservation. There are many bison in zoological gardens throughout the world; however, they are currently not significant as breeding stock for future release.

The Dangers of Domestication

To protect wildlife globally, we need to remove it as a commodity from the marketplace. It is simply not chic, fashionable, or in good taste to misuse wildlife in conspicuous consumption. If we do so, then we in the affluent societies foster wildlife's decimation.

Current international debate about conservation and economics focuses in large part on luxury markets in dead wildlife or on tourism by the affluent and ignores the powerful North American model based on local, populist wildlife harvest

BUFFALO BULL
A massive buffalo bull watches over the rolling prairie grasslands of Theodore Roosevelt National Park in North Dakota. (Photo © Michael H. Francis)

The Return of the Buffalo

When the Creator made the buffalo, he put a power in them. When you eat the meat, that power goes into you, heals the body and spirit. Now we have the poorest diet. We have alcoholism. We have juvenile and adult diabetes. When our spirituality comes back, when we see buffalo as our grandfathers saw them, then we'll be on the road to recovery.
—Les Ducheneaux, former guardian and ceremonial slaughterer of the Cheyenne River buffalo herd, 1994

The revival of the buffalo over the last century stands as a symbol of success in wildlife conservation for North America. It also stands as a symbol of the future to some Native North Americans.

Native North Americans in the United States and Canada stand at the forefront of bison conservation. "The buffalo are vital to our culture," Oglala Sioux Gilbert Mesteth told the Knight-Ridder news service in 1996. Mesteth manages buffalo for the Oglala Sioux parks authority. "Over the years, our culture has started to dwindle. To bring back the buffalo, to make them a central part of our lives again, is important."

Members of several tribes across North America have resurrected herds of buffalo on their lands. From 1992 to 1996, tribes have established fifteen new bison herds and at the same time quadrupled the buffalo population on reservations from two thousand animals to more than eight thousand, roaming over some 100,000 acres [40,000 hectacres] of tribal lands in the United States and Canada. On the Pine Ridge Reservation in South Dakota, the Oglala Sioux have more than doubled the number of buffalo to five hundred in the past four years with plans to have one thousand bison by the year 2000.

The buffalo remains a powerful spirit-animal, and by restoring bison herds on reservations, tribal leaders hope to restore their people's link to their past as a path to start healing the damage from generations of poverty, alcoholism, and spiritual emptiness. "As we bring our herd back to health, we bring our people back to health," says Oglala Sioux buffalo rancher Fred DuBray.

In 1993, the vision of new buffalo herds sparked the creation of the Inter-Tribal Bison Cooperative, which aids tribes and individual buffalo ranchers in their restoration efforts. In 1996, the cooperative counted thirty-three members.

The best news on the conservation front is that more wild, unfenced bison herds have been established in Canada and that wolves have been reintroduced to Yellowstone in the United States. No matter how good the intentions are, holding more bison behind more fences is a stopgap measure at best and not a lasting answer to conservation. The issue remains a volatile and controversial one at the cornerstone of wildlife conservation.

By far the most significant conservation activity pertaining to bison as a genetic resource is taking place in Canada. It is only in Canada that bison and their natural predators have been preserved on large tracts of land, and where reintroductions conserved the natural ecological setting.

In 1994, Native People in Canada won a victory, along with environmental groups and us all: They saved the largest gene pool of the species *Bison bison* from extermination by federal and provincial bureaucracies in Wood Buffalo National Park. For two years now, Cree in northern Alberta have had a voice in bison management.

In the Northwest Territories of Canada all wildlife conservation is under the jurisdiction of Native Canadians. This covers two herds of bison, including the large herd of two thousand buffalo in the Mackenzie lowlands.

The most positive development in bison management in the United States is the reintroduction of wolves to Yellowstone National Park in 1995 and 1996, a step toward restoring the Yellowstone ecosystem. Without its natural predators, bison become domesticated. The wolf reintroduction will make Yellowstone buffalo the only American herd that, by re-adapting to wolf predation, would reverse the effects of inadvertent domestication.

Return of the buffalo
Bison graze amid the steam of hot springs in early winter. To conserve bison as a species, we must conserve their environment—including their predators. Keeping bison in fenced spaces is a stop-gap conservation measure at best. Protected in enclosures, buffalo are inadvertently managed for tractability and are on their way to domestication. This includes weakening or destroying their anti-predator abilities through genetic decay. (Photo © Tom Murphy)

After 1915, we began to go over to Custer, to the buffalo park there. They had a small buffalo herd, and since a lot of townspeople and National Parks Service personnel wanted to see Indians on horseback killing buffalo, they let us shoot a few of them with our bows and arrows.
—Frank Fools Crow

FORAGING HERD
A herd of bison grazes through the grass of Wood Buffalo National Park in Alberta and the Northwest Territories. Bison adapted after the glacial ages to crop prairie vegetation close to the ground. Thus, modern bison have more specialized teeth than their Ice Age ancestors. The Ice Age bison clearly faced less competition for food, as they retained fairly primitive teeth. (Photo © L. N. Carbyn)

and management. The policies governing the laws of North America's wildlife conservation are essentially "tribal" in nature. They are similar to those of Native North Americans as exemplified by how the Labrador Cree manage wildlife: Wildlife is respected and tribally owned, market forces are excluded from its management, allocation is decided by elders after communal discussion and consent, and only the best information by qualified individuals is used in coming to decisions. Annual rounds of public consultation in each state, province, and territory in North America, followed by debate in the legislature, keep wildlife management decisions largely rational but not universally satisfying. Decisions reflect, of necessity, local views and may offend individuals or groups holding different positions. Good examples of this are the "buck law" controversy about whether only male deer may be hunted, and disputes over predator control and reintroduction programs.

The quality of decisions in the North American system depends not only on science, but also on an enlightened public and the political power of special interests groups. Besides the hunting and fishing organizations and the naturalists' and environmental groups, there are animal rights groups bent on eliminating hunting, agricultural bureaucracies bent on game ranching, and affluent hunting fraternities bent on keeping government at arms' length. Understandably, criticism abounds. Unfortunately, although the North American system of wildlife conservation returned wildlife from the verge of extinction while creating economic and employment opportunities, recently its achievements have been ignored, its policies and history forgotten, and years of legislative regionalism and neglect have made it vulnerable to onslaughts.

One of these recent onslaughts is the push to make wildlife, bison included, part of the agricultural enterprise. The policies by which North Americans have conserved wildlife successfully over the past seventy years, and have gained rich economic returns from it, are opposed to those that would make "alternative agriculture" an economic success. Alternative agriculture requires private ownership of wildlife, a market in dead wildlife to sell its products, allocation of wildlife to customers by the pocket book, freedom from restrictive uses of wildlife so that uses or misuses of wildlife become a private matter, and non-interference in decision-making pertaining to the fate of wildlife.

With the promotion by agricultural bureaucracies of alternative agriculture, such as game ranching, the escape of diseases into wild populations of big-game animals from their domesticated counterparts becomes likely. There are a number of reasons for this: The inability of fences to stop the escape of captive wildlife in the long term; the lack of accurate tests for various livestock diseases in wildlife species; inadequate compliance with game-ranch regulations, as well as falsification of veterinary records to boost sales and facilitate cross-border transportation; the failure of quarantine; the large number of small-scale zoos with poor veterinary control that are active traders of captive wildlife; and the involvement of organized crime in the business of procuring and selling wildlife. Bovine tuberculosis quickly spread in the United States and Canada with the onset of game farming. It also spread to humans in unexpected circumstances. Bison in private ownership in the United States were hit particularly hard by tuberculosis transmitted by captive elk. In short, a wildlife farming industry bodes no good for native wildlife populations and poses a perpetual risk to their survival.

Game farming poses more than a disease risk for wildlife. It also leads to genetic pollution when related foreign species or subspecies, or "improved strains" of what was once a wild species, escape and breed with native wildlife to form hybrids.

There are probably more than 100,000 bison on private ranches and Indian reserves under private control and being domesticated for human uses. Any management of wild stock under private control for commerce, such as game ranching, farming, or "trophy breeding," is contrary to conservation. Bison ranching is not conservation; it is domestication, the deliberate or inadvertent alteration of bison to make them tractable and a source of products desired by their owner or the marketplace.

In a very real sense, humans are condemned to art. We simply cannot stop altering whatever we have the power to alter. Thus we take the biological reality of eating and create the ritual of dining. We turn native ecosystems, be they tropical rainforests or deserts, into savannah landscapes of grass and trees. We turn wolves into myriad races of dog, just as we made dozens of domestic chickens from the wild fowl of India. The moment elk ranchers began, they promised to "improve" elk, just as ranchers of other deer species have done in their breeding.

BUFFALO AMONG THE TREES
Bison in Elk Island National Park, Alberta, are held in large paddocks. The northern portion contains offspring of the Pablo-Allard herd that the Canadian government acquired from Montana; the southern portion holds a herd of northern, or "wood," bison. (Photo © Glen and Rebecca Grambo)

*T*here are places set aside for a few surviving buffalo herds in the Dakotas, Wyoming and Montana. There they are watched over by Government rangers and stared at by tourists. If brother buffalo could talk he would say, "They put me on a reservation like the Indians." In life and death we and the buffalo have always shared the same fate.

—*John (Fire) Lame Deer,* Lame Deer Seeker of Visions, *with Richard Erdoes, 1972*

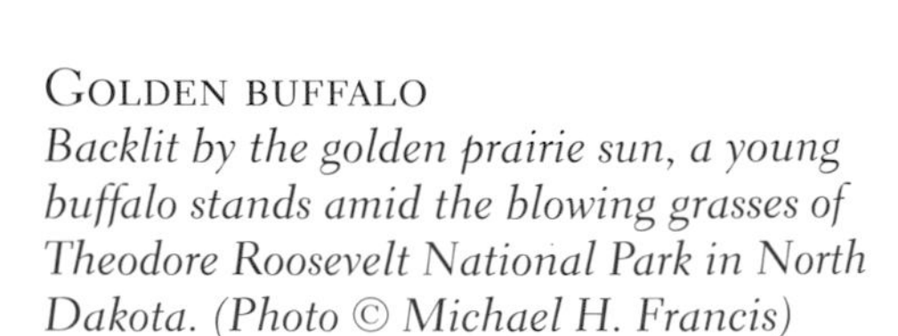

GOLDEN BUFFALO
Backlit by the golden prairie sun, a young buffalo stands amid the blowing grasses of Theodore Roosevelt National Park in North Dakota. (Photo © Michael H. Francis)

We looked upon animals like the wolf, buffalo, elk, and grizzly bear as elders because they were already here in the creation when our people came along. Ours is the task to respect the elders and to respect what the elders teach us.
—*Jack Gladstone, Blackfeet Tribal Council, at a 1992 U.S. Fish and Wildlife Service hearing on reintroducing wolves into Yellowstone*

PEIGAN BUFFALO PICTOGRAPH
A dramatic image of a buffalo bull with heartline painted on a modern Peigan tipi photographed by Liz Bryan in her book, The Buffalo People.

Now it is the bison's turn. In captivity it has been and will again be mongrelized, distorted in body proportions, discolored in its coat, saturated with attention-catching phenodeviants or genetic "oddities," relieved of "wildness" and of any tendency to crash fences and roam by killing off offending bison, bred for long horns and no-horns, bred to become a better converter of feed to flesh, and so on.

The moment bison ranching begins, it generates norms about the shape, size, color, and proportions of buffalo. Such "achievements" generate attention for those that alter the species. It gives them standing among their peers. It permits comparison and ranking. This urge to alter everything that can be controlled is so entirely human, and appears to be so much beyond our ability to suppress, that the only safety for unadulterated wildlife is in public ownership and the prohibition in law of all private ownership. Until then, bison in captivity will be bred to satisfy the whims of customers and owners; they will be domesticated and destroyed as a wild species. Thus while private stocks of wildlife may be in excellent hands and temporarily well conserved and the private initiatives that saved the bison notwithstanding, only public institutions can assure the continuity and comprehensiveness that conservation requires. However, the management of public bison by agencies is not without problems, either.

How secure herds become problem herds has been illustrated in Yellowstone. As long as the bison were confined within the park's borders, the herd generated little controversy. When the herd spilled across the boundaries, major difficulties arose at once. The cause of the dispersal was peculiar and unforeseeable.

Yellowstone began opening its interior to motorized transportation by keeping some roads clear in winter. As the system of roads plowed free of snow or covered by a hard surface groomed to accommodate snowmobiles spread to cover more of the park, bison began to make use of these roads. When snow grew deep, the new roads allowed them to compensate for poor forage by moving to better localities, thus reducing mortality. The bison population grew from about 400 in 1968 to 3,400 in 1993. As bison moved beyond the north and west boundaries of the park, more than 1,127 were shot between 1975 and 1993 in the interest of protecting Montana's livestock industry from brucellosis. Since 1935, the United States has attempted—largely successfully—to eradicate brucellosis from the nation's cattle herds. Many states, including Montana, Wyoming, and Idaho, have been certified as brucellosis free. This status allows the interstate movement of cattle without the need to inspect, test, and quarantine animals for brucellosis. While an infected cattle herd need not be eliminated, the presence of brucellosis imposes a financial burden on the owner and affects the ranch's reputation.

Although only one cattle herd was infected in the vicinity of Yellowstone—a herd that had not been vaccinated against brucellosis—agricultural interests became concerned. In 1988, a lawsuit was filed against Wyoming Game and Fish for $1.2 million in damages by a ranch whose unprotected cattle had developed brucellosis. Brucellosis is carried not only by bison, but also by elk and other wildlife; thus the source of the cattle infection cannot be pinpointed. The suit raised several is-

Return of the buffalo
A herd of buffalo graze over the grasslands of the Wichita Mountains National Wildlife Refuge in Oklahoma in front of an abandoned homestead. (Photo © Jeff and Alexa Henry)

sues, including whether the state must protect private livestock on public land against natural hazards, and the role of private enterprise in protecting its investments by appropriate means. The suit was dismissed. Nevertheless, agricultural interests pushed for a resolution, and a Greater Yellowstone Interagency Brucellosis Committee has been formed to protect the region's elk, bison, and cattle from the disease. The saga of Yellowstone bison and livestock diseases is far from over and, granted the power of agriculture in the United States, the existence of bison is not secure.

The Future of the Buffalo

The bison we know in North America today is a part of a raw, species-poor fauna composed of recently arrived Siberian immigrants, including moose, elk, and grizzly, plus a few surviving species of the old Ice Age fauna, including whitetail and blacktail deer, pronghorn, black bear, and coyote. The new arrivals are none-too-well adapted to the continent's climate and ecological conditions, particularly in the south, nor to one another's diseases, which explains why our wildlife is so susceptible to livestock diseases and to competition. Contrary to popular belief, it is not a long-standing stable ecological situation. The key question for conservationists is which ecosystems and which animal species to preserve.

There is some question as to whether native populations prior to the arrival of

What is life? It is the flash of a firefly in the night. It is the breath of a buffalo in the wintertime. It is the little shadow which runs across the grass and loses itself in the sunset.
—Blackfoot warrior Crowfoot, last words, 1890

BISON SEEKING RESPITE FROM FLIES
Fly-enshrouded bison at Mackenzie Bison Sanctuary in the Northwest Territories. Bison use their tails to deter flies and other insects, a physical adaptation that Indians used to their own benefit in crafting fly swatters from buffalo tails. (Photo © John Dittli)

Columbus were numerous enough to make any difference to the landscape. And if they did make a difference, was it by chance, or was North America at the time of Columbus exploited extensively, but sustainably, by people who were masterful at manipulating the environment to suit their needs?

Two contradictory hypotheses are currently at large. One view contends that native hunters and gatherers lived opportunistically, ruthlessly exploiting all available resources, maximizing short-term utility, and thus had no notion of conservation, let alone management of landscapes for desired resources. The other view is that, despite warfare and strife, native tribes did some good planning and managing to insure a perpetual food supply, by horticultural means for plant food, and by ecological means to insure the availability of animal protein. This theory sees native people as managers of the continent's flora and fauna.

To the arguments pursued here, ironically, it does not really matter which hypothesis is correct. In either case, the continent's flora, fauna, and landscape is the result of human forces—inadvertent in the first hypothesis, deliberate in the second. The landscape is, to a greater or lesser extent, *artificial* in the correct sense of that term: produced by humans to *imitate* nature. Consequently, the pre-Columbian landscape should not be a benchmark for conservation, and to duplicate pre-Columbian conditions, for instance in the small area represented by the Yellowstone ecosystem, is unlikely to maintain viable populations of large animals.

Conservation aims both to prevent species extinction and retain adaptive variation within a species. To do that, conservation must be more than the mere husbanding of species in a zoo or on enclosed pastures. The only constant is change; therefore conservation requires the preservation of environments that continually challenge the adaptations of the species conserved. If this is not done, then these adaptations eventually deteriorate. Worse still, in captivity, selection favors individuals that are adapted not to their native environment but to conditions of captivity. Thus, long-term captivity domesticates. Conservation requires continuity, time, and buffering against capricious change, one reason why private ownership of wildlife is not compatible with conservation.

Historically, the change of wildlife ownership from public to private has led to loss of civil liberties, including the right to bear arms and the right to move freely onto common land now converted to private ownership. Privately owned wildlife has also led to greater hazards as new "wildlife crimes" have been created. The common person has been the loser.

Private ownership of wildlife has also led to capricious genetic manipulation to fulfill market fancies; to the extermination of predators; to loss of species through hybridization; to displacement of native species by competition; to the transfer of diseases and parasites between livestock, wildlife, and humans; to increases in criminal predation on public and private wildlife; and to greater dangers for guardians of wildlife. All this has surfaced in North America with the current upswing in game ranching. In short, the spread of a game farming industry and its link to market economics is a threat to our successes in wildlife management, and constitutes the foremost long-term threat to all wildlife conservation, not just bison conservation.

If bison are to survive in the future, conservation must focus on the long-term maintenance of public bison on public land by public institutions and find a way to deal with agricultural bureaucracies and their call for the destruction of wildlife under the banner of "progress."

A popular view is that conservation requires non-interference with animals in the wild; however, deny the public the use of wildlife and the proprietary interest the public has in wildlife will turn to indifference. Unprotected by an indifferent public, wildlife becomes in reality owned privately—and will be exploited privately for gain. And there is a long, unhappy history of the private use and misuse of wildlife. Like it or not, conservation must be a "hands-on" activity, and not an elimina-

There is a time appointed to all things. Think for a moment how many multitudes of the animal tribes we ourselves have destroyed; look upon the snow that appears today—tomorrow it is water! Listen to the dirge of the dry leaves, that were green and vigorous but a few moons before! We are a part of that life and it seems that our time has come.
—*Lakota Spotted Tail*

tion of all interference with nature. Ideally, it incorporates much "benign neglect" without ever abandoning the readiness to step in correctively at a moment's notice. When powerful cultural activities impinge on nature, there is no alternative but to interfere with natural processes in order to minimize extinctions.

One intriguing suggestion for the future was made by Frank and Deborah Popper in their 1991 article "The Reinvention of the American Frontier" in *The Amicus Journal*. The Poppers propose the reintroduction of an open plain without fences in central North America over which the buffalo can roam once again—a "buffalo commons." After all, the rural economies of the West are declining, as is extractive agriculture. Would we and those that follow us not be better served by a wilderness in the center of the continent, than let the land disappear into private duchies ruled over by the corporate and Hollywood nobility? The Poppers have a case, contentious as it is.

We need to pause and consider what is just ahead, and what it will mean to the conservation of wildlife: ozone depletion and potential burnout of ecosystems by high-energy ultraviolet radiation at high latitudes and altitudes; global warming and

Enduring the winter
A buffalo cow and her calf search for winter forage beneath the snow in Yellowstone National Park. (Photo © Jeff and Alexa Henry)

Buffalo skull
A drawing from the 1910s of a buffalo's last remains by famed photographer Edward S. Curtis.

massive instabilities of climate linked to more destructive weather; the threat of more global pollution as the third world tries to catch up to western standards of affluence; the exponential growth of the global population; and promises of interesting times ahead, particularly two decades from now.

What will we have to do to restore our globe after these agents of destruction have come and gone? Will a Noah's Ark approach to conservation be necessary? Will we have to isolate ourselves and samples of nature from an increasingly hostile physical and social environment, at least temporarily? If we can find a way to protect biodiversity for but another century, we might be in the clear and can restore the biosphere.

The buffalo is a symbol of success in wildlife conservation. It signifies that conservation does work. We have not done gloriously well conserving the bison, but the bison is still with us. It demonstrates that future generations do benefit, that economic, cultural, and scientific options are retained, and that there is hope as we consider ways we can move forward toward healing our planet.

My friend,
They will return again.
All over the Earth,
They are returning again.
Ancient teachings of the Earth,
Ancient songs of the Earth,
They are returning again.
—Oglala Sioux Chief Crazy Horse

Have the spirits let us down? Listen to the prophecies! Next to thirty thousand years, five hundred years look like nothing. The buffalo are returning. They roam off federal land in Montana and Wyoming. Fences can't hold them. Irrigation water for the Great Plains is disappearing, and so are the farmers, and their plows. Farmers' children retreat to the cities. Year by year the range of the buffalo grows a mile or two larger.
—Leslie Marmon Silko, Almanac of the Dead, *1991*

BIBLIOGRAPHY

Pre-Contact Humans and the Buffalo

Birkedale, T. "Ancient Hunters in the Alaskan Wilderness: Human Predators and Their Role and Effect on Wildlife Populations and the Implications for Resource Management." In *Partners in Stewardship: Proceedings of the Seventh Conference Research and Resource Management in Parks and on Public Lands*. Edited by W. E. Brown and S. D. Viers Jr. Hancock, Mich.: George Wright Society, 1993.

Bryan, Liz. *The Buffalo People: Prehistoric Archaeology on the Canadian Plains*. Edmonton: The University of Alberta Press, 1991.

Cohen, M. N. *The Food Crisis in Prehistory*. New Haven, Conn.: Yale University Press, 1977.

Fiedel, S. J. *Prehistory of the Americas*. Cambridge: Cambridge University Press, 1987.

Geist, Valerius. "Neanderthal the Hunter." *Natural History* 90, no. 1 (1981).

Hester, J. J. "The Agency of Man in Animal Extinctions." In *Pleistocene Extinctions*. Edited by P. S. Martin and H. E. Wright Jr. New Haven, Conn.: Yale University Press, 1967.

Speth, J. D. *Bison Kills and Bone Counts*. Chicago: University of Chicago Press, 1983.

Native North Americans and the Buffalo

Ahenakew, Edward. *Voices of the Plains Cree*. Toronto and Montreal: McClelland & Stewart Limited, 1973.

Ambrose, Stephen E. *Crazy Horse and Custer: The Parallel Lives of Two American Warriors*. New York: Meridian, New American Library, 1975.

Connell, Evan S. *Son of the Morning Star: Custer and Little Bighorn*. San Francisco: North Point Press, 1984.

Dion, Joseph F. *My Tribe the Crees*. Calgary, Alberta: Glenbow-Alberta Institute, 1979.

Foster, J. E. "The Métis and the End of Buffalo in Alberta." *Alberta* 3, no. 1 (1992).

Kay, C. E. "Aboriginal Overkill: The Role of Native Americans in Structuring Western Ecosystems." *Human Nature* (in press).

Kennedy, Dan (Ochankugahe). *Recollections of an Assiniboine Chief*. Toronto and Montreal: McClelland & Stewart Limited, 1972.

Lame Deer, John (Fire), and Richard Erdoes. *Lame Deer Seeker of Visions*. New York: Simon and Schuster, 1972.

Linderman, Frank B. *American: The Life Story of a Great Indian, Plenty-coups, Chief of the Crows*. The John Day Company, Inc., 1930.

Long Lance, Buffalo Child. *Long Lance*. New York: Cosmopolitan Book Corporation, 1928.

Mooney, James. *Ghost Dance Religion*. Washington, D.C.: Bulletin of the Bureau of American Ethnology, 43 (1896).

Neihardt, John G. *Black Elk Speaks: Being the Life Story of a Holy Man of the Oglala Sioux*. Lincoln, NE: University of Nebraska Press, 1961.

Oka, Mike. "A Blood Indian's Story" in *The Best from Alberta History*. Hugh Dempsey, ed. Saskatoon, Saskatchewan: Western Producer Prairie Books, 1981.

Standing Bear, Luther. *My Indian Boyhood*. Boston: Houghton Mifflin, 1931.

Standing Bear, Luther. *My People, the Sioux*. Edited by E. A. Brininstool. Boston and New York: Houghton Mifflin, 1928.

Native North American Legends

Bullchild, Percy. *The Sun Came Down: The History of the World as My Blackfeet Elders Told It*. New York: Harper & Row, 1985.

Densmore, Frances. *Teton Sioux Music*. Washington, D. C.: Bulletin of the Bureau of American Ethnology, 61 (1918).

Erdoes, Richard, and Alfonso Ortiz, eds. *American Indian Myths and Legends*. New York: Pantheon Books, 1984.

Petroglyphs and Pictographs

Ewers, John C. *Murals In The Round: Painted Tipis of the Kiowa and Kiowa-Apache Indians*. Washington, D.C.: Smithsonian Institution Press, 1978.

Mallery, Garrick. *Pictographs of the North American Indians*. Washington, D. C.: U.S. Bureau of Ethnology Annual Report, 4 (1882–83).

Rajnovich, Grace. *Reading Rock Art: Interpreting The Indian Rock Paintings Of The Canadian Shield*. Toronto: Natural Heritage/Natural History, Inc., 1994.

Secrist, Kenneth G. *Pictographs in Central Montana*. Missoula, MT: Montana State University, 1960.

North American Explorer Journals and the Buffalo

Bradbury, John. *Bradbury's Travels in the Interior of America 1809–1811*. Early Western Travels, vol. 4. Cleveland, OH: Arthur H. Clark Company, 1904.

Butler, Maj. W. F. *The Great Lone Land: A Narrative of Travel and Adventure in the North-West of America*. London: Sampson Low, Marston, Low, & Searle, 1874.

Catlin, George. *Letters and notes on the manner, customs and conditions of the North American Indians, written during eight years' travel among the wildest tribes of Indians in North America*. New York: Putnam and Wiley, 1841.

Hearne, Samuel. *A Journey from Prince of Wale's Fort in Hudson Bay to The Northern Ocean*. London: 1795.

Henry, Alexander. *New Light on the Early History of the Greater Northwest: The Manuscript Journals of Alexander Henry and of David Th-*

ompson 1799–1814. Elliott Coues, ed. 2 vols. Minneapolis: Ross & Haines, Inc., 1965. Originally published 1897.
Hopwood, V. G. *David Thompson's Travels in Western North America, 1784–1812*. Toronto: Macmillan of Canada, 1971.
Kane, Paul. *Wanderings of an Artist among the Indians of North America*. London: 1859.
Lewis, Meriwether, and William Clark. *The Journals of Lewis and Clark*. Edited by Bernard DeVoto. Boston: The Riverside Press, Houghton Mifflin Company, 1953.
Prince Maximilian zu Wied. "Life Among the Plains Indians in the Final Days of Glory: The Firsthand Account of Prince Maximilian's Expedition Up the Missouri River, 1833–34." In *People of the First Man*. Edited by D. Thomas and K. Ronefeldt. New York: Promontory Press, 1982. Originally published in 1839.

North American Frontier History and the Buffalo

Bryce, George. *The Remarkable History of the Hudson's Bay Company*. London: Sampson Low, Marston & Company, 1900.
Cody, William Frederick (Buffalo Bill). *An Autobiography of Buffalo Bill*. New York: Cosmopolitan Book Corporation, 1920.
Kittredge, William, and Annick Smith. *The Last Best Place: A Montana Anthology*. Helena, MT: The Montana Historical Society Press, 1988.
Lawrence, Bill. *The Early American Wilderness As the Explorers Saw It*. New York: Paragon House, 1991.
McHugh, Tom. *The Time of the Buffalo*. New York: Alfred A. Knopf, 1972.
Sandoz, Mari. *The Buffalo Hunters*. New York: Hastings House, 1954.
Seton, Ernest T. *Lives of Game Animals*. 4 Vols. New York: Doubleday, 1929.
Webb, W. B. *Buffalo Land: An Authentic Account of the Discoveries, Adventures, and Mishaps of a Scientific and Sporting Party with Graphic Descriptions of the Country; the Red Man, Savage and Civilized; Hunting the Buffalo, Antelope, Elk, and Wild Turkey, etc., etc. Replete with Information, Wit, and Humor*. San Francisco: F. Dewing & Co., 1872.
Weekes, Mary. *The Last Buffalo Hunter*. Saskatoon, SK: Fifth House Publishers, 1994. First published by T. Nelson & Sons, New York, 1939.
White, Richard, and Patricia Nelson Limerick. *The Frontier in American Culture*. Berkeley: University of California Press, 1995.

Extermination of the Buffalo

Custer, Gen. George Armstrong. *My Life on the Plains*. 1876.
Custer, Gen. George Armstrong. *Wild Life on the Plains and Horrors of Indian Warfare*. 1891.
Dary, David. *The Buffalo Book: The Full Saga of the American Animal*. N.p.: Swallow Press, Ohio University Press, 1989.
Fehrenbach, T. R. *Lone Star: A History of Texas and Texans*. New York: Collier Books, 1985.
Isenberg, A. "Toward a Policy of Destruction: Buffaloes, Laws, and the Market, 1803–83." *Great Plains Quarterly* 12 (1992).
Rorabacher, J. Albert. *The American Bison in Transition*. St. Cloud, Minn.: North Star Press, 1970.

Saving the Buffalo

Hampton, H. D. *How the U.S. Cavalry Saved our National Parks*. Bloomington: Indiana University Press, 1971.
Hewitt, C. G. *The Conservation of the Wild Life of Canada*. New York: C. Scribner's, 1921.
Hornaday, William T. *The American Natural History*. New York: C. Scribner's, 1904.
Hornaday, William T. *The Extermination of the American Bison, with a Sketch of its Discovery and Life History*. Washington, D.C.: Smithsonian Institution, 1987. Reprint of 1889 edition.
Hornaday, William T. *Our Vanishing Wild Life*. New York: New York Zoological Society, 1913.
Jones, Charles Jesse. *Buffalo Jones' Forty Years of Adventure*. Topeka, Kansas: Crane and Co., 1899.
Lee, W. C. *Scotty Philip: the Man who Saved the Buffalo*. Caldwell, Idaho: Caxton Printers, 1975.

Conservation and the Buffalo

Bean, M. J. *The Evolution of National Wildlife Law*. New York: Praeger, 1983.
Geist, Valerius. "Game Ranching: Threat to Wildlife Conservation in North America." *Wildlife Society Bulletin* 13 (1985).
Geist, Valerius. "How Markets in Wildlife Meat and Parts, and the Sale of Hunting Privileges, Jeopardize Wildlife Conservation." *Conservation Biology* 2, no. 1 (1988).
Geist, Valerius. "Markets in Meat and Parts." In *The Biology of Deer*. Edited by R. D. Brown. New York: Springer-Verlag, 1992.
Highsmith, R. M., et. al. *Conservation in the United States*. Chicago: Rand McNally, 1962.
Martin, Calvin. *Keepers of the Game*. Berkeley: University of California Press, 1978.
Popper, Frank J., and Deborah E. Popper. "The reinvention of the American Frontier." *The Amicus Journal*. Summer (1991).

Art and the Buffalo

Barsness, Larry. *The Bison in Art: A Graphic Chronicle of the American Bison*. Fort Worth, TX: Amon Carter Museum.
Buffalo Bill and the Wild West. Brooklyn, NY: The Brooklyn Museum, 1981.

Natural History and Behavior

Carbyn, L. N., S. M. Oosenburg, and D. W. Anions. *Wolves, Bison, and the Dynamics Related to the Peace-Athabasca Delta in Canada's Wood Buffalo National Park*. Edmonton, Alberta: Canadian Circumpolar Institute, University of Alberta, Circumpolar Research Series No. 4 (1993).
Caughley, G. *The Deer Wars*. Auckland, N.Z.: Heinemann, 1983.
Coder, D. G. "The National Movement to Preserve the American Buffalo in the United States and Canada." Ohio State University, 1975. Unpublished Ph.D. thesis.
Connelly, R. G. , W. Fuller, R. Mercredi, G. Wobeser, and B. Hubert. *Northern Diseased Bison*. Ottawa, Ontario: Federal Environmental Assessment Review Office, Report No. 35 (1990).
Dagg, A. I. *Canadian Wildlife and Man*. Toronto: McClelland & Stewart, 1974.
Dehn, M. M. "Vigilance for Predators: Detection and Dilution Effects." *Behavioural Ecology and Sociobiology* 26 (1990).

Flores, D. "Bison Ecology and Bison Diplomacy: The Southern Plains from 1800–1850." *Journal of American History* 78, no. 2 (1991).

Fuller, W. A. "The Biology and Management of Bison of Wood Buffalo National Park." *Wildlife Management Bulletin* 1 (16).

Gambaryan, P. P. *How Animals Run*. New York: John Wiley & Sons, 1974.

Garretson, M. S. *The American Bison*. New York: New York Zoological Society, 1938.

Geist, Valerius. "Adaptive Behavioral Strategies." In *Elk of North America*. Edited by J. W. Thomas and D. E. Toweill. Harrisburg, Penn.: Stackpole Books, 1982.

Geist, Valerius. "Behavior: Adaptive Strategies in Mule Deer." In *Mule and Black-Tailed Deer of North America*. Edited by O. C. Wallmo. Lincoln, Neb.: Wildlife Management Institute, University of Nebraska Press, 1981.

Geist, Valerius. "Bergmann's Rule Is Invalid." *Canadian Journal of Zoology* 65 (1987).

Geist, Valerius. "Bones of Contention Revisited: Did Antlers Enlarge with Sexual Selection as a Consequence of Neonatal Security Strategies?" *Applied Animal Behaviour Science* 29 (1991).

Geist, Valerius. "A Comparison of Social Adaptations in Relation to Ecology in Gallinaceous Bird and Ungulate Societies." *Annual Review of Ecology and Systematics* 8 (1977).

Geist, Valerius. "Culture and its Biological Origin." In *The Ethological Roots of Culture*. Edited by R. A. Gardner, et. al. The Netherlands: Kluwer, 1994.

Geist, Valerius. "Did Predators Keep Humans out of North America?" In *The Walking Larder: Patterns of Domestication, Pastoralism, and Predation*. Edited by J. Clutton-Brock. One World Archeology, Vol. 2. London: Unwin Hyman, 1989.

Geist, Valerius. "The Evolution of Horn-like Organs." *Behaviour* 27 (1966).

Geist, Valerius. "How Bison Live." *Alberta* 3, no. 2 (1993).

Geist, Valerius. *Life Strategies, Human Evolution, Environmental Design*. New York: Springer-Verlag, 1978.

Geist, Valerius. "New Evidence of High Frequency Antler Wounding in Cervids." *Canadian Journal of Zoology* 64 (1986).

Geist, Valerius. "On reproductive strategies in ungulates and some problems of adaptation." In *Evolution Today: Proceedings of the 2nd International Congress of Systematics and Evolutionary Biology*. Edited by G. G. E. Scudder and J. L. Reveal. Pittsburgh, Penn.: Carnegie-Mellon University, 1981.

Geist, Valerius. "The Paradox of the Great Irish Stag." *Natural History* 95, no. 3 (1986).

Geist, Valerius. "Phantom Subspecies." *Alberta* 3, no. 2 (1993).

Geist, Valerius. "The Relation of Social Evolution and Dispersal in Ungulates During the Pleistocene, with Emphasis on the Old World Deer and the Genus *Bison*." *Quaternary Research* 1 (1971).

Geist, Valerius, and M. Bayer. "Sexual Dimorphism in the Cervidae and its Relation to Habitat." *Journal of Zoology*. London, 214 (1988).

Geist, Valerius, and P. T. Bromley. "Why Deer Shed Antlers." *Zeitschrift für Saugetierkunde* 43 (1978).

Geist, Valerius, and P. Karsten, "The Wood Bison (*Bison athabascae* Rhoads) in Relation to Hypotheses on the Origin of the American Bison (*Bison bison* Linnaeus)." *Zeitschrift für Saugetierkunde* 42 (1977).

Guthrie, R. D. "Mosaics, Allochemics, and Nutrients. An Ecological Theory of Late Pleistocene Megafaunal Extinctions." In *Quaternary Extinctions*. Edited by P. S. Martin and R. G. Klein. Tucson, Ariz.: University of Arizona Press, 1984.

Guthrie, R. D. *Frozen Fauna of the Mammoth Steppe*. Chicago: University of Chicago Press, 1989.

Haynes, G. "Toothwear in Bison." *Journal of Mammalogy* 65 (1984).

Kurten, Bjoern, and E. Anderson. *Pleistocene Mammals of North America*. New York: Columbia University Press, 1980.

Maegher, Dr. Mary. "Winter Recreation-induced changes in bison numbers and distribution in Yellowstone National Park." Unpublished paper.

Maegher, Dr. Mary. "Evaluation of Boundary Control for Bison of Yellowstone National Park." *Wildlife Society Bulletin* 17 (1989).

Maegher, Dr. Mary. "Range Expansion by Bison of Yellowstone National Park." *Journal of Mammalogy* 70 (1989).

Martin, P. S., and J. E. Guilday. "Bestiary for Pleistocene Biologists." In *Pleistocene Extinctions*. Edited by P. S. Martin and H. E. Wright. New Haven, Conn.: Yale University Press, 1967.

Northern Diseased Bison Environmental Assessment Panel of Environment Canada. *Dealing with the Diseases of Bison in Northern Canada*. Newsletter No. 1, January 1989.

Owen-Smith, R. N. *Megaherbivores*. Cambridge: Cambridge University Press, 1988.

Owen-Smith, Norman. "Pleistocene Extinctions: The Pivotal Role of Megaherbivores." *Paleobiology* 13 (1987).

Pattie, O. G., in *Man Meets Grizzly*. Edited by F. H. Young and C. Beyers. Boston: Houghton Mifflin, 1980.

Peden, D. G., and G. J. Kraay. "Comparison of Blood Characteristics in Plains Bison, Wood Bison and Their Hybrids," *Canadian Journal of Zoology* 57 (1979).

Pielou, E. C. *After the Ice Ages*. Chicago: University of Chicago Press, 1991.

Roe, Frank Gilbert. *The North American Buffalo*. Toronto: University of Toronto Press, 1951.

Soper, J. D. "History Range, and Home Life of the Northern Bison." *Ecological Monographs* 11 no. 4 (1941).

Stahl, D. *Wild, Lebendige Umwelt* (Freiburg: Alber, 1979).

van Camp, J. D. "A Surviving Herd of Endangered Wood Bison at Hook Lake, N.W.T.?" *Arctic* 42, no. 4 (1989).

Van Valdenburgh, B., and F. Hertel. "Tough Times at La Brea: Tooth Breakage in Large Carnivores of the Late Pleistocene." *Science* 261 (1993).

Van Vuren, D. "Bison West of the Rocky Mountains: An Alternative Explanation." *Northwest Science* 61 (1987).

Van Zyll de Jong, C. G. *A Systematic Study of Recent Bison with Particular Consideration of the Wood Bison*. Publications in Natural Sciences No. 6. Ottawa, Ontario: National Museum of Canada, 1986.

INDEX

About the Author

As a child, Valerius Geist had an all-consuming interest in animals. He made numerous sketches of animals and spent as much time as possible in the forest observing and dreaming. He yearned to become a scientist who studied animals, and eventually he did.

His career as a zoologist has taken him to many wild places and to meet many of the world's greatest naturalists. He spent nearly two years in isolation in northern Canada studying mountain sheep and goats, living in a small cabin and not seeing another human being for months on end. He tamed wild animals in the wild; at one point, bighorn females tried to retain him physically in their bands, and the males attacked him.

He has focused on how animals communicate, the nature of aggression, and on status displays, and his mountain sheep work has become well known. His interests extended to the evolution of Ice Age mammals, and later to humans, when he became the first Program Director of Environmental Science in a new Faculty of Environmental Design at the University of Calgary, Alberta, Canada. Here he focused on generating environments that maximize human health and developed a biological theory of health. He continued to be interested in wild creatures, but turned from academic to applied science and to wildlife conservation policy.

After twenty-seven years as a professor, Valerius retired to pursue his other interests and to enjoy family life. He and his wife, Renate, have three children and two grandchildren.

Valerius Geist is also the author of *Mule Deer Country*, *Elk Country*, *Wild Sheep Country*, and *Mountain Sheep*, for which he won the 1972 Book of the Year Award from The Wildlife Society. He has been a consultant to the National Geographic Society on several books and television specials. How to retain Earth's biodiversity beyond the impending human population wave is his concern for the future.